All in a Row

moda All-Stars

All in a Row

24 Row-by-Row Quilt Designs

Compiled by Lissa Alexander

Martingale®
Create with Confidence

Moda All-Stars All in a Row: 24 Row-by-Row Quilt Designs
© 2015 by Martingale & Company®

Martingale®
19021 120th Ave. NE, Ste. 102
Bothell, WA 98011-9511 USA
ShopMartingale.com

Printed in China

20 19 18 17 16 15   8 7 6 5 4 3 2 1

Library of Congress Cataloging-in-Publication Data available upon request.

ISBN: 978-1-60468-729-3

MISSION STATEMENT
Dedicated to providing quality products and service to inspire creativity.

CREDITS

PUBLISHER AND CHIEF VISIONARY OFFICER
Jennifer Erbe Keltner

EDITORIAL DIRECTOR
Karen Costello Soltys

MANAGING EDITOR
Tina Cook

ACQUISITIONS EDITOR
Karen M. Burns

TECHNICAL EDITOR
Laurie Baker

COPY EDITOR
Sheila Chapman Ryan

DESIGN DIRECTOR
Paula Schlosser

PHOTOGRAPHER
Brent Kane

PRODUCTION MANAGER
Regina Girard

ILLUSTRATOR
Rose Wright

Dedication

With special thanks to Mark Dunn and Cheryl Freydberg
for discovering and nurturing the talent in all of us.

To standing with other quilters, all in a row,
and making sure no child begins or ends
the day hungry. Let's make the world
a more beautiful place together.

All royalties for this book will be donated
to No Kid Hungry (nokidhungry.org),
a charitable organization dedicated
to ending childhood hunger.

Contents

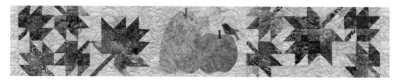

Classic Patchwork

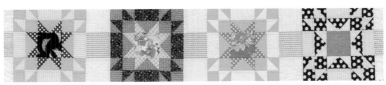

We're at our best together!

Quilting is all about making it personal—choosing the colors you like, the designs that make your heart sing, the patterns that seem perfect for your fabrics. And with a row quilt, you don't have to make too many of any one thing. Every row is a new adventure. That's why I think the idea of making row quilts has become so popular once again.

I'm always on the lookout for ways to bring together the talented team of Moda Fabric designers. Individually, you know and love their work. But it's rare when we all get to work together for a common goal. I'm thrilled to share the work that 24 of Moda Fabric's All-Stars teamed up to create— a one-of-a-kind collection of quilt rows for you to choose from. We divided the rows into three groups—whimsical, seasonal, and classic—and added in several spacer rows. But there are no rules about how you combine them. Feel free to mix and match them to meet your heart's desire and end up with a quilt that's all your own!

And as you row along, know that your purchase of this book is also doing good things to end childhood hunger among US public schoolkids. Together, the designers are all donating their royalties from this book's sales to benefit No Kid Hungry (nokidhungry.org)—a charitable organization dedicated to ending childhood hunger through school breakfast programs.

Together, all in a row, we as quilters stand together to make life better! Now let's get rowing along....

—Lissa Alexander

HERE'S THE *Skinny* FROM THE ALL-STARS

As you peruse the pages of this book, you'll see columns just like this one sprinkled throughout. What you'll find in them are little pieces of info and advice from each of the All-Star designers. Their personalities shine through, so you're likely to find a kindred spirit in these pages. After all, they may be All-Star fabric designers, but they're also passionate quilters, just like you!

Here are the sentences we asked them to complete:

- **I'm currently obsessed with** _____.

- **If I'm not quilting, I'm** _____.

- **The best piece of advice (regarding quilting) I've received was** _____.

- **My go-to snack food for a full day (or night) of quilting is** _____.

- **When I just can't get a quilt to come together,** _____.

- **My go-to color combination is** _____.

- **I can't begin a new quilting project unless** _____.

- **On my playlist while I'm quilting is** _____.

- **Beyond designing, my favorite part of making a quilt is** _____.

- **One little tip that will make creating my row better, easier, or more accurate is** _____.

Join the fun. What would your answers be?

9

Sing Your Song

Designed by Sandy Klop of American Jane Patterns

Combine colorful scraps of classic paisleys, checks, and pindots to create this folksy appliqué row featuring a bluebird singing a springtime serenade.

Finished row: 9½" x 48"

Materials

Yardage is based on 42"-wide fabric. Fat quarters are 18" x 21".

1½ yards of off-white print for background

1 fat quarter of green paisley for vine

8" x 8" square *each* of 2 coordinating medium-green prints for leaf appliqués

7" x 7" square of red checkerboard for extra-large heart appliqué

3" x 12" rectangle of black solid for music-note appliqués

Scraps of 4 assorted blue prints for bird lower body, bird upper body, bird wing, and large heart appliqués

Scraps of 2 red prints for medium heart and circle appliqués

Scraps of 2 yellow prints for small heart and beak appliqués

¼ yard of 17"-wide lightweight paper-backed fusible web

Black embroidery floss

Size 26 hand-embroidery needle

Water- or air-soluble fabric marker

Cutting

All measurements include ¼"-wide seam allowances.

From the *lengthwise grain* of the off-white print, cut:

1 strip, 10" x 48½"

From the *bias* of the green paisley, cut:

Enough 1⅛"-wide strips to equal at least 54" when joined end to end

Appliqué the Row

For additional information on appliqué and embroidery techniques, go to ShopMartingale.com/HowtoQuilt.

1 Join the green paisley bias strips end to end to make a strip at least 54" long. Fold the strip in half lengthwise, wrong sides together. Stitch the long raw edges together. Center the seam on the back of the strip and press the seam allowances open.

2 Fold the off-white print strip in half crosswise and lightly finger-press the fold to mark the center. Refer to the placement diagram to pin the vine in place, seam side down. Appliqué the vine in place using your favorite method.

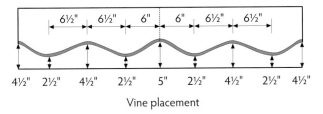

Vine placement

3 Using the patterns below and on page 12, prepare the shapes for fusible appliqué. Position the prepared shapes on the background strip, referring to the photo on page 10 as needed. Follow the manufacturer's instructions to fuse the shapes in place. Machine stitch around each appliqué using a zigzag stitch, blanket stitch, or the stitch of your choice to permanently attach the shape to the background strip.

4 Use the bird pattern and fabric marker to transfer the eye placement and leg lines to the appliquéd bird. Using one strand of black floss and the embroidery needle, backstitch the bird's legs and make two straight stitches, side by side, for the eye.

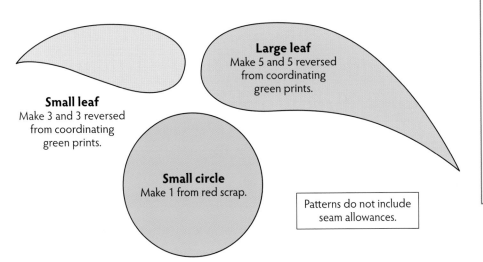

Small leaf
Make 3 and 3 reversed from coordinating green prints.

Large leaf
Make 5 and 5 reversed from coordinating green prints.

Small circle
Make 1 from red scrap.

Patterns do not include seam allowances.

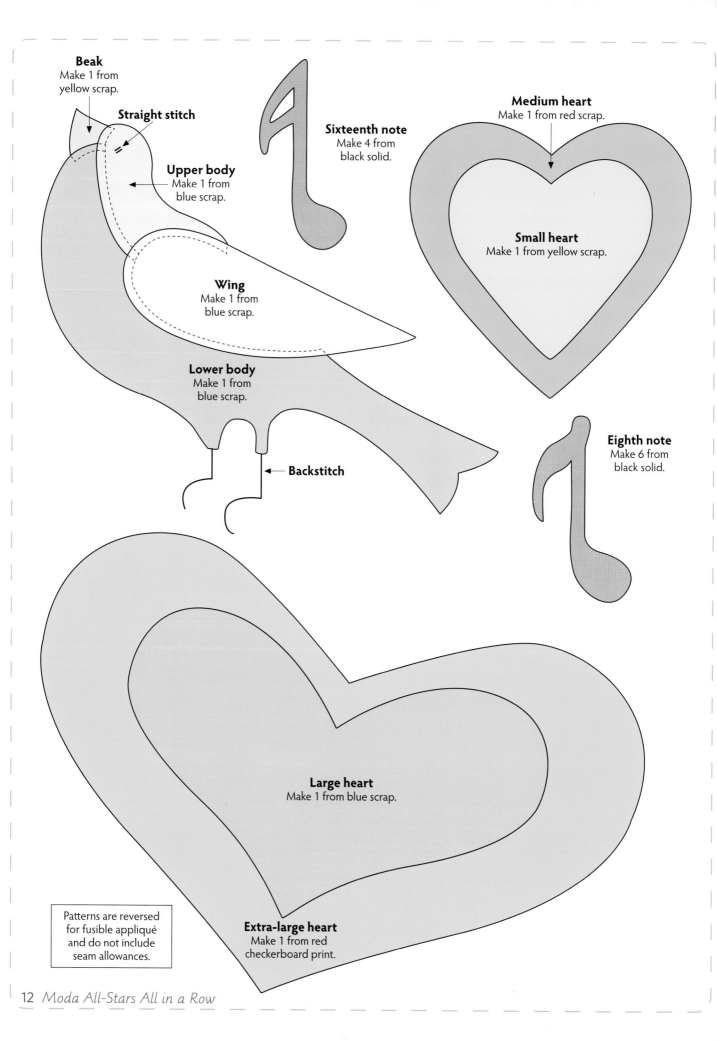

Beak
Make 1 from yellow scrap.

Straight stitch

Sixteenth note
Make 4 from black solid.

Medium heart
Make 1 from red scrap.

Upper body
Make 1 from blue scrap.

Small heart
Make 1 from yellow scrap.

Wing
Make 1 from blue scrap.

Lower body
Make 1 from blue scrap.

Eighth note
Make 6 from black solid.

Backstitch

Large heart
Make 1 from blue scrap.

Patterns are reversed for fusible appliqué and do not include seam allowances.

Extra-large heart
Make 1 from red checkerboard print.

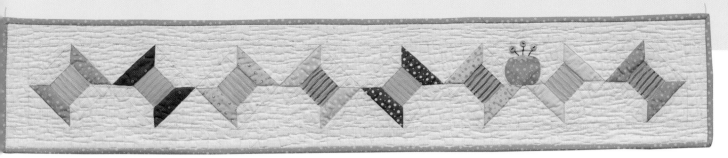

Thread and Pincushion

Designed by Sandy Gervais of Pieces from My Heart

Take inspiration from your sewing room and stitch a row of cute Spool blocks set on point. Continue the theme by adding a sweet appliquéd pincushion.

Finished row: 8⅝" x 48"

Materials

Yardage is based on 42"-wide fabric.

⅝ yard of mint print for background

4" x 5" rectangle *each* of 8 assorted polka dots for spools

6" x 6" square *each* of 3 assorted stripes for thread

4" x 4" square of lightweight paper-backed fusible web

3" x 5" rectangle of red polka dot for pincushion-body and center appliqués

1" x 1½" rectangle of green print for pincushion-top appliqué

Black embroidery floss

Size 24 hand-embroidery needle

3 assorted buttons, ⅜" diameter

Water- or air-soluble fabric marker

Cutting

All measurements include ¼"-wide seam allowances.

From the mint print, cut:

3 strips, 2" x 42". From *1 of the strips,* cut 2 rectangles, 2" x 6⅛".
   Set aside the remainder of the strip for the border.

3 strips, 1½" x 42"; crosscut into:
   16 rectangles, 1½" x 2½"
   32 squares, 1½" x 1½"

4 squares, 7" x 7"; cut into quarters diagonally to yield 16 side
   setting triangles (you'll use 14 and have 2 left over)

2 squares, 3¾" x 3¾"; cut in half diagonally to yield 4 corner
   setting triangles

From *each* of the 8 assorted polka dots, cut:

2 rectangles, 1½" x 4½" (16 total)

From *each* of the 3 assorted stripes, cut:

3 squares, 2½" x 2½" (9 total)

Sandy combines her love for art, color, and quilting in her fabric and patterns to bring new adventure to a time-honored tradition through her Pieces from My Heart business (piecesfrommyheart.net).

- **I'm currently obsessed with** anything watercolor.

- **If I'm not quilting, I'm** painting.

- **The best piece of advice (regarding quilting) I've received was** unless it's a 4-H project, it doesn't have to be perfect. The goal is to finish.

- **My go-to snack food for a full day (or night) of quilting is** chocolate, salt, chocolate, salt....

- **When I just can't get a quilt to come together,** I put it in the "too ugly to live" bin. Every once in a while, I will make a collage picture using the "too ugly to live" quilt blocks. Surprisingly enough, the project usually turns out pretty cool.

- **My go-to color combination is** red and something.

- **I can't begin a new quilting project unless** I tidy up my studio somewhat (emphasis on somewhat!).

- **On my playlist while I'm quilting is** nothing. I never listen to music.

- **Beyond designing, my favorite part of making a quilt is** binding, because the end is near!

- **One little tip that will make creating my row better is** to use connector squares, also called flip and sew, or folded corners, which result in fewer seams.

Make the Spool Blocks

1 Draw a diagonal line from corner to corner on the wrong side of each mint 1½" square. Place a marked square on one end of a polka-dot 1½" x 4½" rectangle as shown. Stitch on the marked line. Trim ¼" from the stitching line. Press the seam allowances toward the corner. Repeat on the opposite end of the rectangle to make a spool unit. Repeat with the remaining polka-dot rectangles and marked mint squares to make a total of 16 units.

Make 16.

2 With the stripes running horizontally, sew mint 1½" x 2½" rectangles to the sides of a striped 2½" square. Press the seam allowances toward the square. Repeat to make a total of eight thread units. You'll have one striped square left over.

Make 8.

3 Sew matching spool units to the top and bottom of a thread unit as shown. Press the seam allowances toward the thread unit. Repeat to make a total of eight blocks.

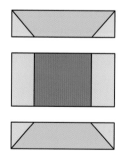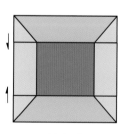

Make 8.

Assemble the Row

1 Arrange the blocks and mint side setting triangles into eight diagonal rows, rotating the blocks as shown. Stitch the setting triangles to the blocks. Press the seam allowances toward the setting triangles.
Sew the rows together. Press the seam allowances in one direction.
Add the corner triangles to the ends. Press the seam allowances toward the triangles.

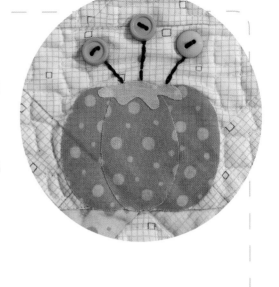

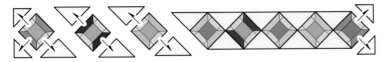
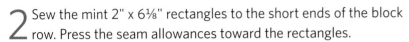

2 Sew the mint 2" x 6⅛" rectangles to the short ends of the block row. Press the seam allowances toward the rectangles.

3 Cut the short mint 2"-wide strip in half crosswise. Sew one half to one end of each mint 2" x 42" strip. Trim each pieced strip to 2" x 48½". Sew these strips to the top and bottom of the block row.

Add the Details

For additional information on appliqué and embroidery techniques, go to ShopMartingale.com/HowtoQuilt.

1 Use the patterns below to prepare the shapes for fusible appliqué. Position the prepared shapes on the background strip, referring to the photo on page 13 as needed. Follow the manufacturer's instructions to fuse the shapes in place. Stitch around each appliqué using a zigzag stitch, blanket stitch, or the stitch of your choice to permanently attach the shapes to the background strip.

2 Use the pattern and the fabric marker to transfer the pin shaft lines above the appliquéd pincushion. Using four strands of black floss and the embroidery needle, backstitch the pin shafts. Stitch a button to the end of each embroidered pin shaft.

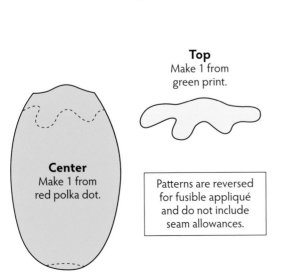

Center
Make 1 from
red polka dot.

Top
Make 1 from
green print.

Patterns are reversed
for fusible appliqué
and do not include
seam allowances.

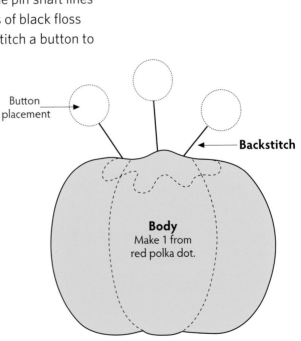

Button
placement

Backstitch

Body
Make 1 from
red polka dot.

Wash Day

Designed by Pat Sloan

Finished row: 10" x 48"

Select cheerful scraps to make a fun and fanciful row featuring laundry hanging out to dry in the breeze.

Materials

Yardage is based on 42"-wide fabric.

½ yard of pink-on-white print for background

⅛ yard of pink polka dot for sashing

Scraps of assorted blue, green, and yellow prints for appliqués

½ yard of 17"-wide lightweight paper-backed fusible web

2 yards of blue jumbo rickrack

Water- or air-soluble fabric marker

Cutting

All measurements include ¼"-wide seam allowances.

From the pink-on-white print, cut:

3 rectangles, 10½" x 15½"

From the pink polka dot, cut:

2 strips, 2" x 10½"

Assemble and Appliqué the Row

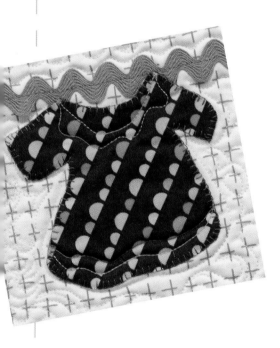

1 Alternately sew the pink-on-white rectangles and pink polka-dot sashing strips together as shown. Press the seam allowances toward the sashing strips.

2 Fold the background strip in half crosswise and lightly finger-press the fold to mark the center. Referring to the photo on page 16, use the fabric marker to draw two curved lines on the background to mark the rickrack placement, starting each line along the top edge at the center point and ending about 1½" from the corner. Cut a piece of rickrack the length of each drawn line. Place a piece of rickrack over each drawn line, and then pin or baste it in place. Stitch through the center of the rickrack lengths to secure them to the background.

3 Using the patterns on pages 18–20, prepare the shapes for fusible appliqué. For more information on fusible appliqué, go to ShopMartingale.com/HowtoQuilt, or see Pat's book *Teach Me to Appliqué* (Martingale, 2015). Position the top edges of the clothing shapes on the rickrack and center the large heart about 1" from the bottom edge of the strip, referring to the photo as needed. Center the medium heart over the large heart. Follow the manufacturer's instructions to fuse the shapes in place. Stitch around each shape using a zigzag stitch, blanket stitch, or the stitch of your choice to permanently attach the appliqués to the background strip.

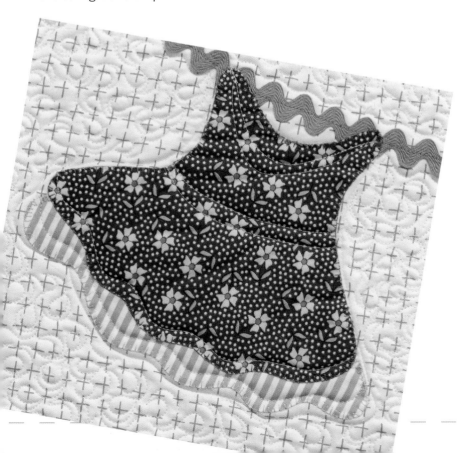

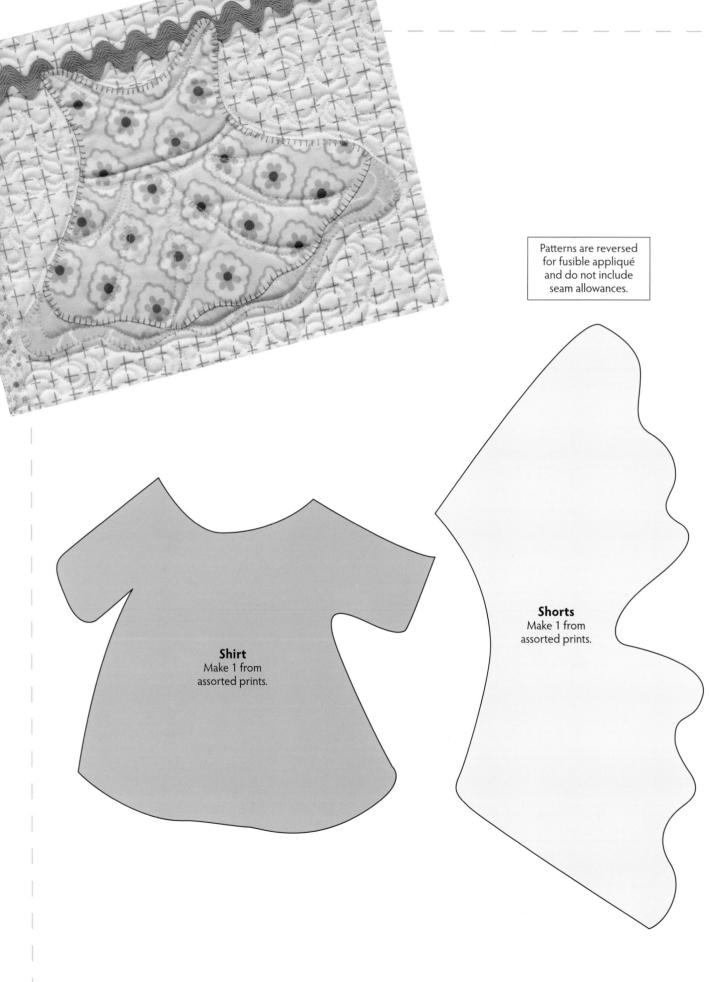

Patterns are reversed
for fusible appliqué
and do not include
seam allowances.

Shirt
Make 1 from
assorted prints.

Shorts
Make 1 from
assorted prints.

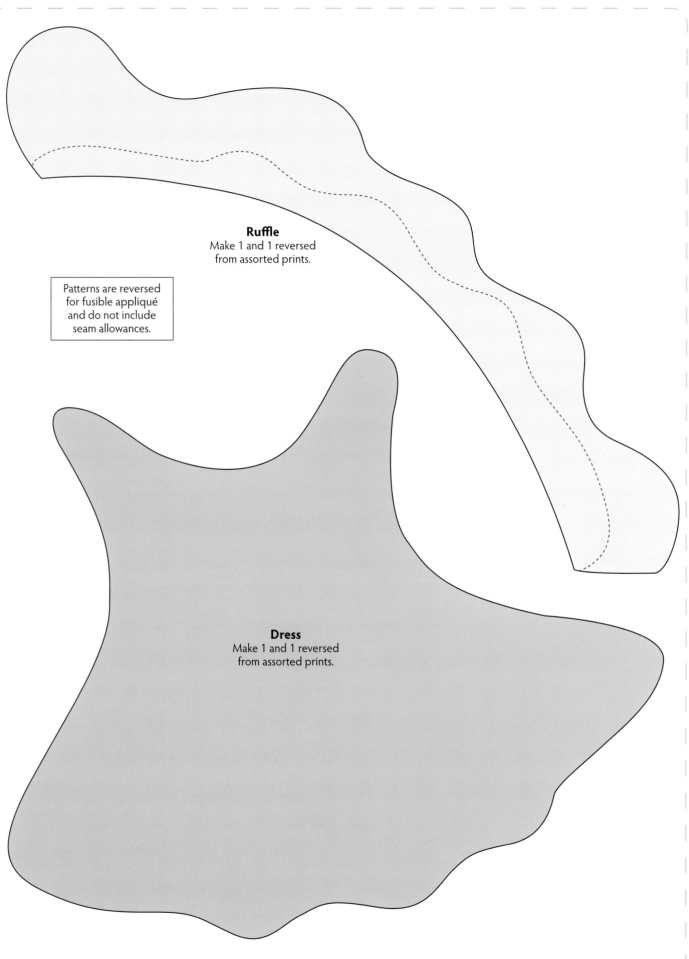

Ruffle
Make 1 and 1 reversed
from assorted prints.

Patterns are reversed
for fusible appliqué
and do not include
seam allowances.

Dress
Make 1 and 1 reversed
from assorted prints.

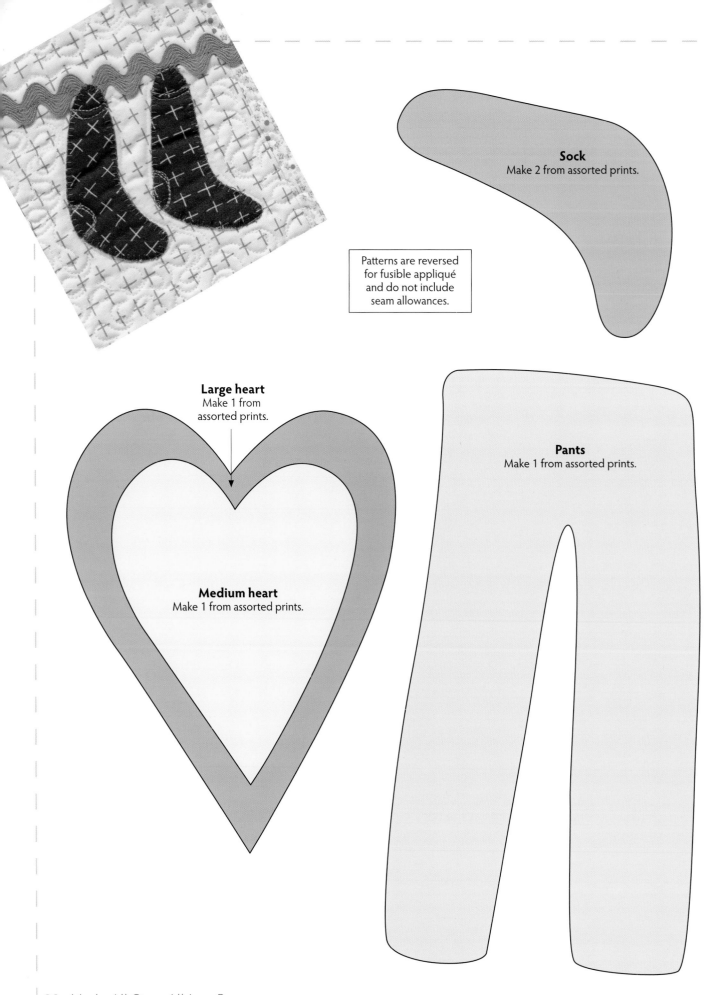

Sock
Make 2 from assorted prints.

Patterns are reversed
for fusible appliqué
and do not include
seam allowances.

Large heart
Make 1 from
assorted prints.

Pants
Make 1 from assorted prints.

Medium heart
Make 1 from assorted prints.

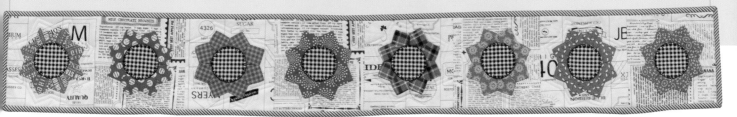

Bloom

Designed by **Karla Eisenach of Sweetwater**

Mix red, black, and white prints to sew a row of appliqué blossoms that's sweet in its simplicity.

Finished row: 6" x 48"

Materials

Yardage is based on 42"-wide fabric. Fat eighths are 9" x 21".

½ yard of white type print for background
2" x 42" strip *each* of 8 assorted red prints for flower petals
1 fat eighth of black gingham for flower centers
⅛ yard of 17"-wide lightweight paper-backed fusible web
Template plastic
Black embroidery floss
Size 24 hand-embroidery needle

Cutting

All measurements include ¼"-wide seam allowances. Trace the flower-petal pattern on page 23 onto template plastic and cut it out. Use the template to cut the flower-petal pieces from the red strips as indicated below.

From the white type print, cut:
2 strips, 6½" x 42"; crosscut into 8 squares, 6½" x 6½"
From *each* of the 8 assorted red strips, cut:
8 flower petals (64 total)

Make the Flower Blocks

1 Fold a flower petal in half lengthwise, right sides together. Stitch across the wide end, backstitching at the beginning and end. Trim away the seam allowance at the fold to reduce bulk, being careful not to cut into the stitching.

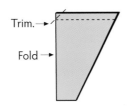

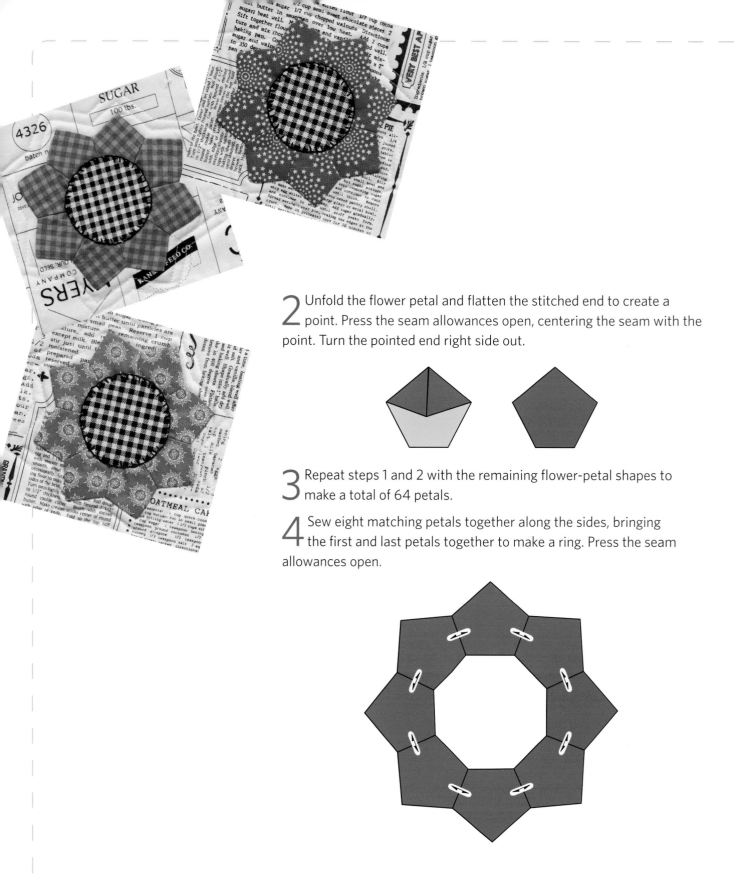

2 Unfold the flower petal and flatten the stitched end to create a point. Press the seam allowances open, centering the seam with the point. Turn the pointed end right side out.

3 Repeat steps 1 and 2 with the remaining flower-petal shapes to make a total of 64 petals.

4 Sew eight matching petals together along the sides, bringing the first and last petals together to make a ring. Press the seam allowances open.

5 Fold a 6½" square in half vertically and horizontally and lightly finger-press the folds. Open up the square. With right sides up, center a petal ring on the square, aligning the petal seams at the side and top and bottom with the fold lines; pin in place. Using a blind stitch and matching thread, sew around the outer edges of the ring.

6 Using the pattern below, prepare the flower centers for fusible-web appliqué. For additional information on appliqué and embroidery techniques, go to ShopMartingale.com/HowtoQuilt.

7 Center a prepared shape on each flower ring, covering the raw ends of the petals. Follow the manufacturer's instructions to fuse the shapes in place. Using three strands of floss and the embroidery needle, blanket stitch around the edges of each center circle.

Assemble the Row

Join the eight blocks side by side. Press the seam allowances in one direction.

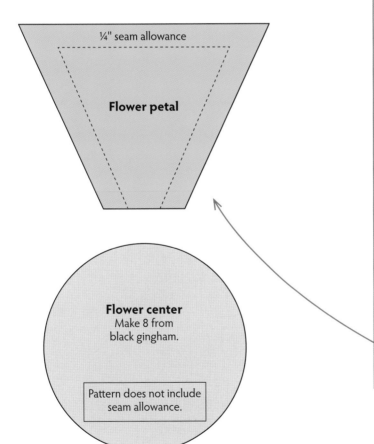

¼" seam allowance

Flower petal

Flower center
Make 8 from
black gingham.

Pattern does not include
seam allowance.

HERE'S THE
Skinny
FROM KARLA EISENACH

Sweetwater is a family-run design company in Colorado (thesweetwaterco.com). The company is a spin-off of Karla's original pattern company, Farmyard Creations.

- **I'm currently obsessed with** home decorating.

- **If I'm not quilting, I'm** cleaning.

- **The best piece of advice (regarding quilting) I've received was** press seams open.

- **My go-to snack food for a full day (or night) of quilting is** chocolate.

- **When I just can't get a quilt to come together,** I start all over—many of my projects end up getting tossed.

- **My go-to color combination is** red and white.

- **I can't begin a new quilting project until** I have a clean space.

- **On my playlist while I'm quilting is** *Fixer Upper* on HGTV.

- **Beyond designing, my favorite part of making a quilt is** binding. Because it means I am finished!

- **One little tip that will make creating my row easier is** to use the flower-petal template (above left) to make the flower petals.

Snowy Day

Designed by Anne Sutton of Bunny Hill Designs

Finished row: 10" x 48"

Piecing and appliqué join forces with a touch of embroidery to make this cozy winter scene.

Materials

Yardage is based on 42"-wide fabric. Fat eighths are 9" x 21".

¼ yard *each* of tan-on-white polka dot and red tree print for blocks

¼ yard *each* of green snowflake print, white-and-green stripe, and white tree print for background

1 fat eighth *each* of green skate print and white-and-red stripe for background

1 fat eighth of red skate print for background and star appliqué

⅛ yard of off-white solid for snowman appliqués

5" x 5" square of red plaid for scarf and stocking-hat appliqués

4" x 4" square of tan print for scarf and stocking-hat cuff appliqués

3" x 3" square of tan polka dot for stovepipe-hat appliqués

Orange, black, and brown embroidery floss

Size 26 hand-embroidery needle

2 black buttons, ¼" diameter

Water- or air-soluble fabric marker

Cutting

All measurements include ¼"-wide seam allowances.

From the tan-on-white polka dot, cut:
6 squares, 4" x 4"
12 squares, 2½" x 2½"

From the red tree print, cut:
6 squares, 4" x 4"
3 squares, 2½" x 2½"

From the green snowflake print, cut:
1 rectangle, 6½" x 7½" (A)
1 rectangle, 3" x 9½" (B)
1 rectangle, 2¾" x 7" (C)

1 rectangle, 2½" x 16½" (D)
1 rectangle, 1½" x 6½" (E)
1 rectangle, 1¼" x 7" (F)
1 rectangle, 1" x 6½" (G)

From the white-and-green stripe, cut:
1 rectangle, 7½" x 9½" (H)
1 rectangle, 2½" x 12½" (I)

From the white tree print, cut:
1 rectangle, 7½" x 8½" (J)
1 rectangle, 2½" x 7½" (K)
1 rectangle, 1½" x 6½" (L)

From the green skate print, cut:
1 rectangle, 4½" x 9½" (M)

From the white-and-red stripe, cut:
1 rectangle, 1½" x 16½" (N)

From the red skate print, cut:
2 rectangles, 1½" x 16½" (O)

Make the Ohio Star Blocks

1 Draw a diagonal line from corner to corner on the wrong side of each tan-on-white polka-dot 4" square. Layer a marked square on top of each red tree print 4" square, right sides together. Stitch ¼" from each side of the marked lines. Cut the squares apart on the marked lines to make two half-square-triangle units from each pair (12 total). Press the seam allowances toward the red.

Make 12.

2 Layer two half-square-triangle units right sides together, with the red fabric halves on the polka-dot halves. On the top unit, draw a line from corner to corner in the opposite direction from the seam line. Stitch ¼" from each side of the marked line, and then cut the squares apart on the marked line to make two quarter-square-triangle units. Repeat with the remaining units from step 1 to make a total of 12 quarter-square-triangle units. Press the seam allowances in either direction. Square up each unit to 2½" x 2½".

Make 12.

3 Arrange four quarter-square-triangle units, four tan-on-white polka-dot 2½" squares, and one red tree print 2½" square in three horizontal rows as shown. Sew the pieces in each row together. Press the seam allowances toward the squares. Sew the rows together. Press the seam allowances toward the middle row. Repeat to make a total of three blocks. The blocks should measure 6½" x 6½".

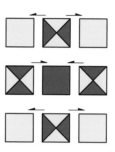

Make 3.

Assemble the Row

When assembling the sections, press the seam allowances toward the newly added rectangle after each one is added.

1 To make section 1, sew the G rectangle to the top of a block. Join the C and F rectangles to the sides of the block. Add the B rectangle to the bottom of this unit, and then add the H rectangle to the right edge. Sew an O rectangle to the bottom of the unit.

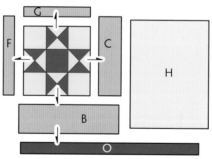

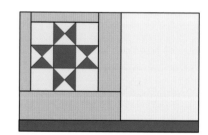

Section 1

2 To make section 2, sew the L rectangle to the top of a block. Join the J and K rectangles to the sides of the block. Add the D rectangle to the bottom of this unit, and then add the N rectangle to the bottom of the D rectangle.

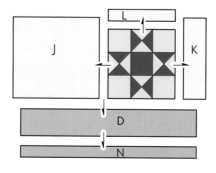

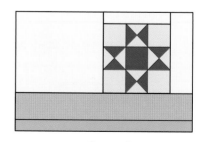

Section 2

3 To make section 3, sew the E rectangle to the bottom of the remaining block. Join the A rectangle to the right edge. Add the I rectangle to the top of this unit, and then add the M rectangle to the left edge. Sew the remaining O rectangle to the bottom of the unit.

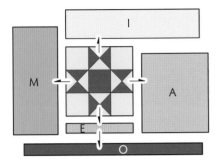
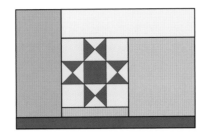

Section 3

4 Join the sections. Press the seam allowances toward sections 1 and 3.

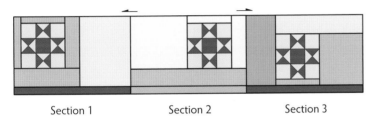

Section 1   Section 2   Section 3

Appliqué the Row

1 Using the patterns on page 28, prepare the shapes for turned-edge appliqué. For more information on turned-edge appliqué, go to ShopMartingale.com/HowtoQuilt.

2 Using the photo on page 24 as a guide, position the snowman appliqués on the background so they will be "sitting" on the bottom seamline when finished. Appliqué the scarf and hat shapes to the snowmen. Position and appliqué the star between the second and third snowmen.

Add the Details

1 Referring to the photo as needed, use the arm embroidery pattern and the fabric marker to mark each snowman's arms.

2 Using two strands of floss and the embroidery needle, embroider the details as follows.

   Noses: Outline with orange floss and a tiny backstitch, and then fill in with satin stitch.

   Arms: Stem-stitch with brown floss.

   Eyes: Three-wrap French knot with black floss.

   Buttons: Cross-stitch with black floss.

3 Quilt the row, and then sew a button to the top of the stocking hats.

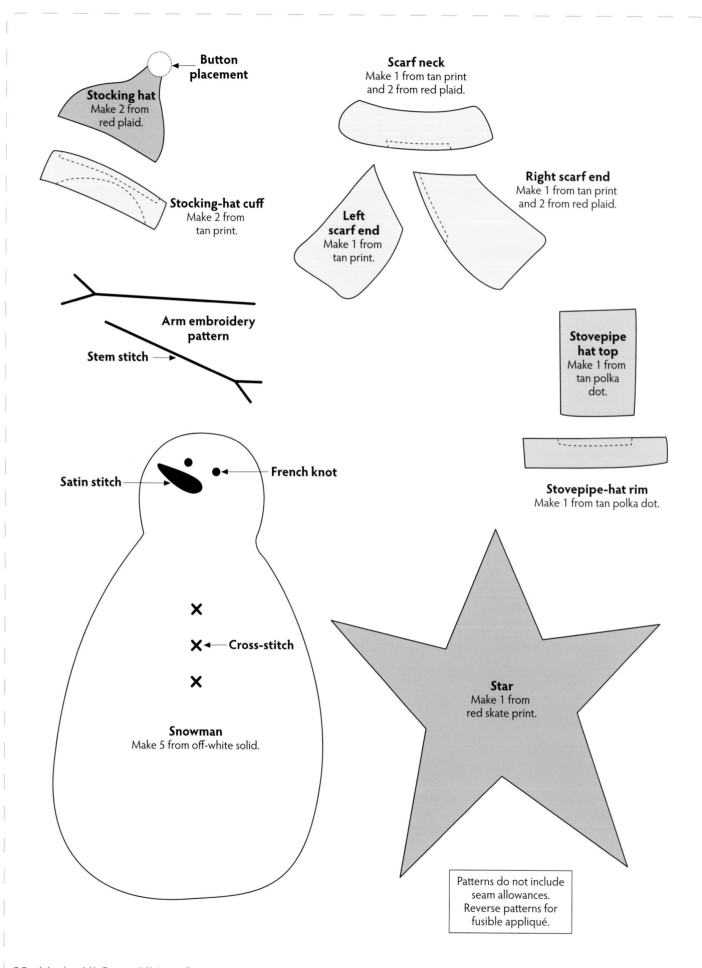

Button placement

Stocking hat
Make 2 from red plaid.

Stocking-hat cuff
Make 2 from tan print.

Scarf neck
Make 1 from tan print and 2 from red plaid.

Left scarf end
Make 1 from tan print.

Right scarf end
Make 1 from tan print and 2 from red plaid.

Stovepipe hat top
Make 1 from tan polka dot.

Stovepipe-hat rim
Make 1 from tan polka dot.

Arm embroidery pattern

Stem stitch

Satin stitch

French knot

Cross-stitch

Snowman
Make 5 from off-white solid.

Star
Make 1 from red skate print.

Patterns do not include seam allowances. Reverse patterns for fusible appliqué.

Fetch

Designed by Barbara Groves and Mary Jacobson

Pretty pinwheels careen between two playful pups on a charming patchwork row.

Finished row: 10" x 48"

Materials

Yardage is based on 42"-wide fabric.

¾ yard of white solid for background

2½" x 2½" square *each* of 18 assorted pink, yellow, orange, blue, purple, and turquoise prints for Pinwheel blocks

7" x 7" square *each* of black print #1 and black print #2 for Dog blocks

2" x 3" rectangle *each* of red print #1 and red print #2 for Dog blocks

Scraps of assorted green prints for grass strip

Cutting

All measurements include ¼"-wide seam allowances.

From the white solid, cut:

2 strips, 3½" x 42"; crosscut into:
    7 rectangles, 3½" x 4½"
    4 rectangles, 2½" x 3½"

2 strips, 2½" x 42"; crosscut into 18 squares, 2½" x 2½"

6 strips, 1½" x 42"; crosscut *3 of the strips* into:
    10 rectangles, 1½" x 7½"
    2 rectangles, 1½" x 2"
    22 squares, 1½" x 1½"

2 rectangles, 2¾" x 3"

2 rectangles, 2½" x 4¾"

2 rectangles, 2¼" x 3¼"

2 rectangles, 1¼" x 2¼"

2 rectangles, 1¼" x 1½"

2 rectangles, 1¾" x 7½"

From *each* of the 2 black prints, cut:

1 rectangle, 2½" x 3" (2 total)

1 rectangle, 2" x 2¼" (2 total)

4 squares, 1¼" x 1¼" (8 total)

(Continued on page 30)

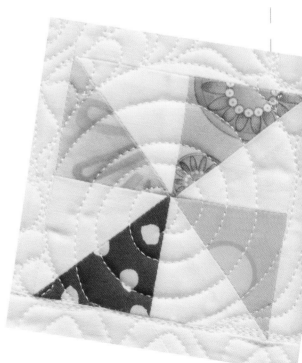

Sisters Barbara Groves and Mary Jacobson once owned a quilt shop. Designing and sewing samples was more fun than they could imagine, so they sold the store and began creating patterns and fabric for Me and My Sister Designs (meandmysisterdesigns.com).

- **I'm currently obsessed with** knitting (Mary).

- **If I'm not quilting, I'm** reading (Barb).

- **The best piece of advice (regarding quilting) I've received was** "Always listen to my sister" (Barb).

- **My go-to snack food for a full day (or night) of quilting is** Hershey's Nuggets, milk chocolate with almonds and toffee (Barb). Gummy bears! They have to be Haribo (Mary).

- **When I just can't get a quilt to come together,** I slam a door or two (Barb). I put it away forever (Mary).

- **My go-to color combination is** turquoise and green (Barb). Pink and green (Mary).

- **I can't begin a new quilting project unless** I tidy up my sewing room (Barb and Mary).

- **On my playlist while I'm quilting is** reality TV! I watch it all! From *Ink Master* to *Survivor* to *Project Runway* (Barb). *Downton Abbey;* I'm on season three (Mary).

- **Beyond designing, my favorite part of making a quilt is** hand sewing the binding (Barb). Cutting! (Mary).

- **One little tip that will make creating our row easier is** to press the seams open (Mary).

(Continued from page 29)

From *each* of the 2 red prints, cut:
2 squares, 1¼" x 1¼" (4 total)

From the assorted green scraps, cut:
23 squares, 1½" x 1½"

Make the Dog Blocks

Press the seam allowances open.

1 Using the 1¼" squares, draw a diagonal line from corner to corner on the wrong side of two black #1 squares, two black #2 squares, and both red print #1 and #2 squares.

2 Place the marked black #1 square on the right end of a white 1¼" x 2¼" rectangle as shown. Stitch on the marked line. Trim ¼" from the stitching line; press. Repeat with the marked black #2 square to make a mirror-image unit. Place the black square on the left of the remaining white rectangle and orient the marked line as shown.

Make 1 of each.

3 Place a marked red #1 square on the upper-right corner of a white 2¼" x 3¼" rectangle as shown. Stitch, trim, and press as before. Repeat to make a mirror-image unit, placing a red #2 square on the upper-left corner of the remaining white rectangle and orienting the marked line as shown.

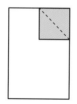   

Make 1 of each.

4 Place the remaining marked red #1 and black #1 squares on the lower corners of a white 2¾" x 3" rectangle as shown. Stitch, trim, and press as before. Repeat to make a mirror-image unit, placing the remaining marked red #2 and black #2 squares on opposite corners.

Make 1 of each.

5 Sew matching black 1¼" squares to the sides of a white 1¼" x 1½" rectangle. Repeat to make a total of two units.

Make 2.

6 Using black #1 and red #1 pieces, arrange the units from steps 2–5, the black 2" x 2¼" rectangle, and the black 2½" x 3" rectangle into two vertical rows as shown. Join the pieces in each row; press. Sew the rows together to make the left-facing Dog block; press.

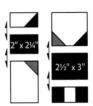 

7 Using black #2 and red #2 pieces, repeat step 6 with the remaining units from steps 2–5 and the remaining black 2" x 2¼" and 2½" x 3" rectangles, arranging the pieces as shown to make the right-facing Dog block.

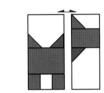

8 Sew a white 2½" x 4¾" rectangle to the top of each block; press. Add a white 1¾" x 7½" rectangle to the tail side of each block; press.

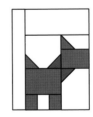 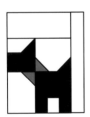

Make the Pinwheel Blocks

1 Draw a diagonal line from corner to corner on the wrong side of each white 2½" square. Layer a marked square on top of each of the pink, yellow, orange, blue, purple, and turquoise 2½" squares, right sides together. Sew ¼" from both sides of the marked line. Cut the squares apart on the marked line to make two half-square-triangle units from each pair of squares (36 total). Press the seam allowances toward the colored triangles. Square up each unit to 2" x 2".

Make 36.

2 Arrange four different half-square-triangle units in two rows of two units each as shown. Sew the units in each row together. Press the seam allowances in opposite directions. Sew the rows together and press the seam allowances open. Repeat to make a total of nine Pinwheel blocks. The blocks should measure 3½" x 3½".

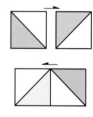

Make 9.

Assemble the Row

1 Arrange the Dog blocks, the Pinwheel blocks, and the white 1½"x 7½", 3½" x 4½", and 2½" x 3½" rectangles into a row as shown. Sew the white 3½" x 4½" and 2½" x 3½" rectangles to the Pinwheel blocks first, and then sew the 1½" x 7½" rectangles to those units. Add the Dog blocks to the ends of the row last.

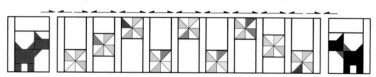

2 To make the grass strip, alternately join the green and white 1½" squares side by side with green squares at both ends; press. Add a white 1½" x 2" rectangle to each end of the row; press.

1½" x 2"   1½" x 2"

3 Join the three remaining white 1½" x 42" strips end to end to make one long strip. From the pieced strip, cut two strips, 1½" x 48½". Sew these strips to the top and bottom edges of the grass strip; press.

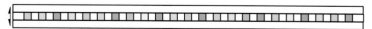

4 Sew the grass strip to the bottom of the block strip; press toward the grass strip.

Bird on a Pumpkin

Designed by Edyta Sitar of Laundry Basket Quilts

Combine patchwork and appliqué to make a row featuring colorful tumbling leaves and a little feathered friend perched on a plump pumpkin.

Finished row: 9" x 48"

Materials

Yardage is based on 42"-wide fabric.

⅝ yard *total* of assorted light batik scraps for Leaf blocks
⅜ yard *total* of assorted dark batik scraps for Leaf blocks
6" x 9" rectangle of orange batik for tall pumpkin appliqué
6" x 6" square of dark-orange batik for short pumpkin appliqué
2" x 3" rectangle of brown batik #1 for stem appliqués
2" x 3" rectangle of blue batik for bird bottom appliqué
2" x 3" rectangle of brown batik #2 for bird top appliqué
Brown fine-tip permanent marker (optional)

Cutting

All measurements include ¼"-wide seam allowances.

From the assorted light batik scraps, cut a *total* of:
2 squares, 3½" x 3½"
24 squares, 2⅜" x 2⅜"; cut in half diagonally
    to yield 48 triangles
108 squares, 2" x 2"

**From the assorted dark batik scraps,
    cut a *total* of:**
24 squares, 2⅜" x 2⅜"; cut in half diagonally
    to yield 48 triangles
34 squares, 2" x 2"
24 squares, 1¼" x 1¼"
2 rectangles, 1" x 5½"
8 rectangles, 1" x 3½"

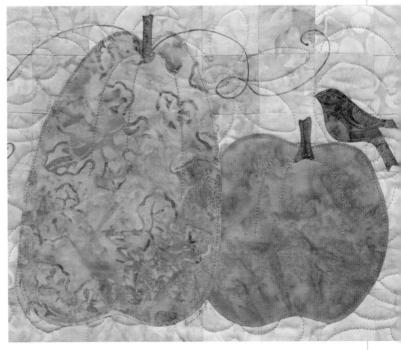

Make the Leaf Blocks

1 Arrange four dark 1¼" squares into two vertical rows of two squares each. Sew the squares in each row together. Press the seam allowances in opposite directions. Join the rows. Press the seam allowances open. Repeat to make a total of six four-patch units.

Make 6.

2 Sew a light triangle to a dark triangle along the long edges to make a half-square-triangle unit. Press the seam allowances toward the dark. Repeat to make a total of 48 units.

Make 48.

3 To make the stem units for the small Leaf blocks, select eight light 2" squares and cut them in half diagonally. Sew the halves back together, inserting a dark 1" x 3½" rectangle between the triangles. Press the seam allowances toward the stem strips. Square up the units to 2" x 2". In the same manner, cut the two light 3½" squares in half and insert a dark 1" x 5½" rectangle between the triangles; press and trim as before to make the stem units for the large Leaf blocks. Square up the units to 3½" x 3½".

Make 8.

Make 2.

4 To make the small Leaf blocks, lay out three dark 2" squares, four half-square-triangle units, one light 2" square, and one small stem unit into three horizontal rows as shown. Sew the pieces in each row together. Press the seam allowances in the direction indicated. Sew the rows together. Press the seam allowances open. Repeat to make a total of eight small Leaf blocks, randomly substituting a four-patch unit for one of the dark 2" squares in four of the blocks.

Make 8.

5 To make the large Leaf blocks, lay out seven dark 2" squares, one four-patch unit, eight half-square-triangle units, five light 2" squares, and one large stem unit into four rows as shown, randomly placing the four-patch unit in any position where a dark square is shown. Sew the units in the first three rows together. Press the seam allowances in the direction indicated. For the bottom row, join the units to the right of the stem unit into two short rows, pressing the seam allowances as indicated, and then sew the rows together. Add the stem unit to the left edge of the joined rows to complete the bottom row. Sew the rows together. Press the seam allowances open. Repeat to make a total of two blocks.

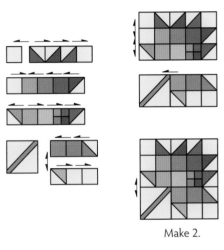

Make 2.

Make the Appliquéd Block

1 Refer to step 1 of "Make the Leaf Blocks" to make 15 four-patch units using four light 2" squares for each unit.

2 Lay out the four-patch units in four vertical rows of three units each. Sew the units in each row together. Press the seam allowances open. Join the rows and press the seam allowances open.

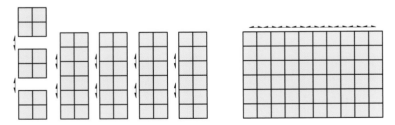

3 Using the patterns on pages 37 and 38, prepare the shapes for fusible appliqué. For more information on fusible appliqué, go to ShopMartingale.com/HowtoQuilt. Referring to the photo on page 33 as needed, position the short pumpkin, and then the tall pumpkin on the pieced background from step 2. Add the stems to each pumpkin.

Position the bird on the short pumpkin. Follow the manufacturer's instructions to fuse the shapes in place. Stitch around each appliqué using a straight stitch, zigzag stitch, blanket stitch, or the stitch of your choice to permanently attach the shape to the background strip.

4 If desired, use the fine-tip marker to draw the vine off the stem of the tall pumpkin. Or, mark the vine with a water- or air-soluble marker and embroider the detail.

Assemble the Row

1 Sew five light 2" squares together side by side to make a row. Press the seam allowances in the direction indicated. Repeat to make a total of two rows. Sew a row to the top of each large Leaf block. Press the seam allowances open.

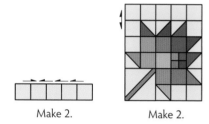

Make 2.   Make 2.

2 Lay out the large and small Leaf blocks and the appliquéd block in seven vertical rows as shown. Sew the small Leaf blocks together in pairs. Press the seam allowances open. Join the rows. Press the seam allowances open.

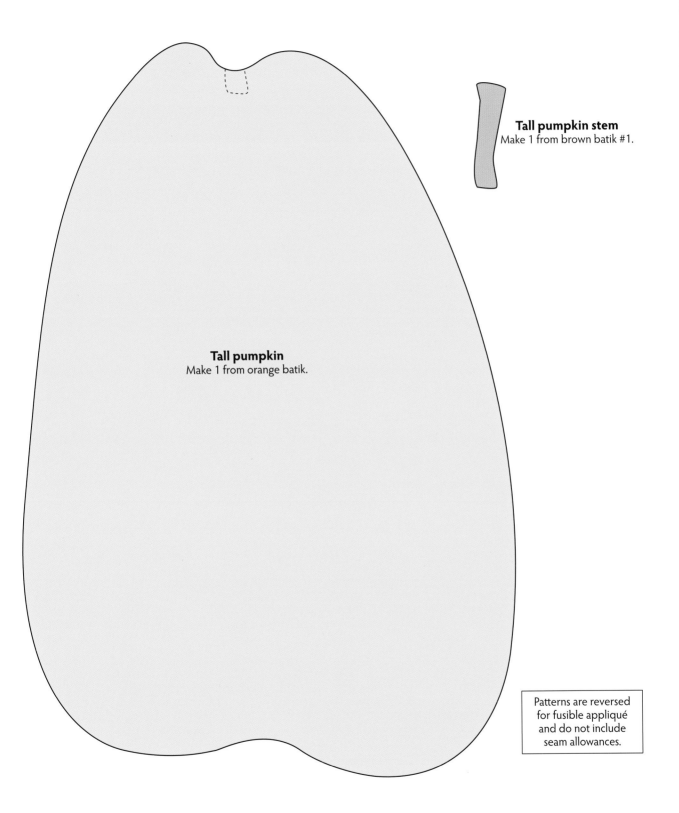

Tall pumpkin stem
Make 1 from brown batik #1.

Tall pumpkin
Make 1 from orange batik.

Patterns are reversed
for fusible appliqué
and do not include
seam allowances.

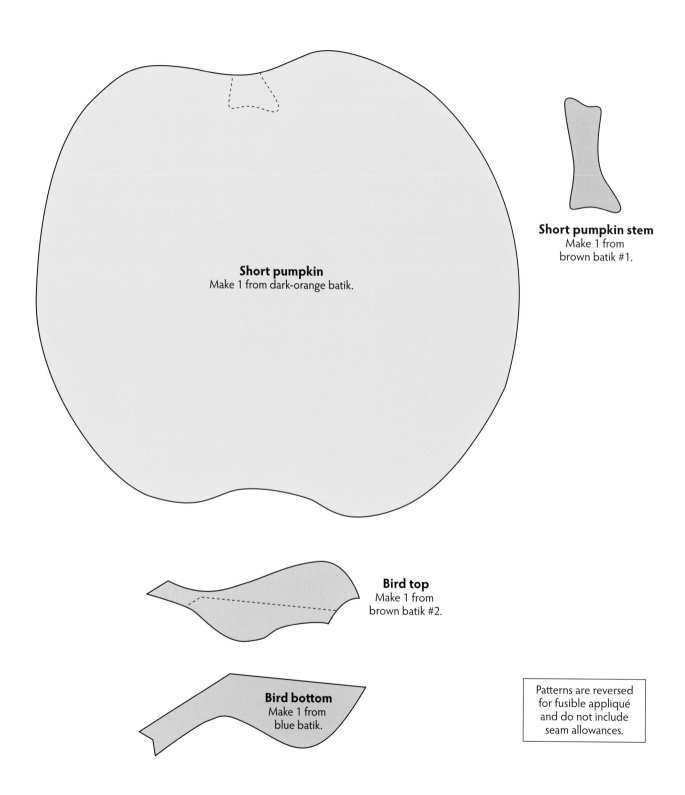

Short pumpkin
Make 1 from dark-orange batik.

Short pumpkin stem
Make 1 from
brown batik #1.

Bird top
Make 1 from
brown batik #2.

Bird bottom
Make 1 from
blue batik.

Patterns are reversed
for fusible appliqué
and do not include
seam allowances.

Row Houses

Designed by Carrie Nelson

Finished row: 10" x 48"

Mix and match floral, checked, polka-dot, and graphic-print scraps to create a village of cozy cottages.

Materials

Yardage is based on 42"-wide fabric.

½ yard *total* of assorted medium and dark prints for houses
⅓ yard of white print for background
⅛ yard *total* of assorted green prints for grass
Water- or air-soluble fabric marker

Cutting

All measurements include ¼"-wide seam allowances.

From the white print, cut:

1 square, 10" x 10"
14 squares, 3½" x 3½"
7 rectangles, 2½" x 6½"

From the assorted medium and dark prints, cut a *total* of:

7 rectangles, 3½" x 6½" (or, to make a pieced roof like some of the houses shown, sew two strips together and trim to 3½" x 6½")
7 rectangles, 2½" x 3½"
7 strips, 2½" x 13"; crosscut *each strip* into:
    2 rectangles, 2½" x 5" (14 total)
    1 rectangle, 2" x 2½" (7 total)

From the assorted green prints, cut a *total* of:

1 rectangle, 2½" x 10"
7 rectangles, 2½" x 6½"

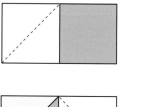
Make the House Blocks

1 Draw a diagonal line from corner to corner on the wrong side of each white print 3½" square. Lay a marked square on one end of a medium or dark print 3½" x 6½" rectangle, right sides together as shown. Sew on the marked line. Trim ¼" from the stitching line. Press the seam allowances toward the corner. Lay another marked square on the opposite end of the rectangle as shown; stitch, trim, and press as before to make a flying-geese unit for the roof. Repeat to make a total of seven roof units.

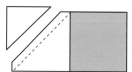

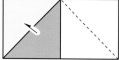

Make 7.

2 Sew a medium or dark 2" x 2½" house rectangle to the top of a 2½" x 3½" door rectangle. Press the seam allowances toward the house rectangle. Sew matching 2½" x 5" house rectangles to the sides of the unit. Press the seam allowances toward the house rectangles. Repeat to make a total of seven house units.

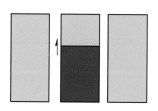

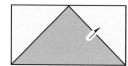

Make 7.

3 Sew a roof unit to the top of each house unit. Press the seam allowances open. Join an assorted green 2½" x 6½" rectangle to the bottom of each unit. Press the seam allowances open. Add a white 2½" x 6½" rectangle to the top of each unit. Press the seam allowances open.

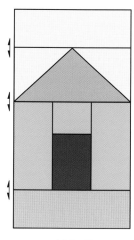

Make 7.

Assemble the Row

To give the finished row the up-and-down look, the house blocks are offset slightly. The assembled row is then trimmed. These instructions include the layout for the row with the placement of the spacer pieces and the offset increments of the blocks, but this is just a starting point. Feel free to change, adjust, or eliminate the pieces to get the look you want. If you change the offset, keep in mind that there's only 1½" to play with. The row will be trimmed to measure 10½" tall.

1. Sew the green 2½" x 10" strip to the bottom of the white 10" square to make a strip set. Press the seam allowances open. Crosscut the strip set into two 2"-wide spacer segments and three 1½"-wide spacer segments as shown, left.

2. Lay out the blocks and spacer segments as shown, offsetting the blocks as indicated or as desired. Sew the pieces together. Press the seam allowances as indicated.

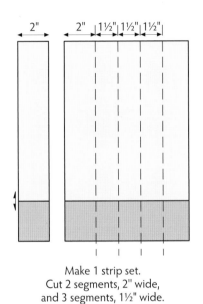

Make 1 strip set.
Cut 2 segments, 2" wide,
and 3 segments, 1½" wide.

The finished width of the spacers adds up to the width of one house block, so if you eliminate the spacers, you can add an eighth house.

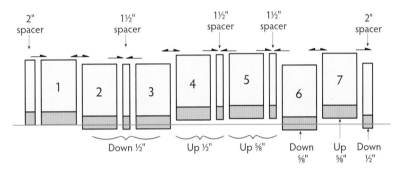

3. Using a long ruler and the fabric marker, mark the top edge of the strip across the lowest point, using the seamlines between the blocks and spacer segments as a guideline for keeping the edge straight. Measure 10½" from the top edge to mark the bottom edge of the strip. If you're happy with the placement lines, cut along the marked lines. If not, you should have some wiggle room to adjust the lines down a bit.

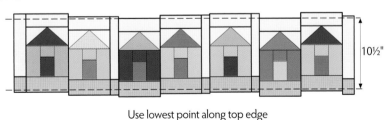

Use lowest point along top edge
to mark entire top edge.

Gallery of Row Quilts

Where do I begin when making a row quilt? How many rows should it be? What colors should I choose? To provide a few of the answers to jump-start your thinking, here's a gallery of ideas and photographs. Want more inspiration? Join the Moda All-Stars All in a Row Quilt-Along Facebook Group. Tag your projects from the book with #allinarowquiltalong.

FACING PAGE: One secret to successfully piecing a row quilt together is to allow a little breathing room between the showstopper rows. To do that, place narrow spacer rows in between. Piecing the spacer rows, rather than inserting a plain strip of sashing, helps unify the look of the finished quilt.

This quilt includes the following rows: "Bloom," "Rail Fence" blender row, "Garland Knot," "Hourglass" bender row, "He Loves Me...," "Flying Geese" blender row, "Sing Your Song," "Four Patch" blender row, and "Meadow Rose."

Pieced by Sarah Huechteman; quilted by Maggi Honeyman

Don't limit yourself by thinking that the rows in this book must be combined to make great quilts. If you have a favorite row, you can piece, quilt, and bind it, and then use the small piece in unexpected ways throughout your home.

LEFT: Turn "Twinkle" into the perfect skinny quilt to fit in a narrow vertical spot next to an entryway door or window. What could be more inviting?

BELOW RIGHT: Or take the narrow "Bloom" row and wind it through an artful display of your favorite collection, such as this shelf of cream pottery.

ABOVE: Repetition in shape and color is a decorating rule of thumb that's easy to remember and easy to implement. "Garland Rows," with its heart motif made from a twining vine, pairs perfectly when tucked above a table decorated with a vine topiary. The sweet white blooms mimic the lightness of the row's background. The dots of pink in the prints are repeated in small accents with pink-tipped flowers and buds.

LEFT: No room for a 48"-wide row quilt on your walls? No worries! Take the elements you like and create your own custom-sized row quilt.

"Meadow Rose Variation" pieced by Sarah Huechteman; quilted by Maggi Honeyman

ABOVE: Feather your nest by layering a single finished row such as the "Double Star" atop linen or burlap fabric in a tabletop display. Adding decorative items with varied textures and materials creates a look rich and warm.

Have you ever passed over a pattern because you didn't care for the color choices? Here's proof that color can make all the difference in what a pattern looks like. These two quilts use identical feature rows and swap out a few different spacer rows, but the similarities in this pair stop there. A scrappy mix of happy colors blends the diversity of rows well in the version on the left. Trimming down the palette to prints in only two colors creates more definition and contrast between elements in the version on the right. What's your favorite combination?

LEFT: This quilt includes the following rows: "We Are Family," "Flying Geese" blender row, "Wash Day," "Four Patch" blender row, "Twinkle," "Rail Fence" blender row, "Row Houses," and "Flying Geese" blender row.

ABOVE: The quilt above includes the following rows: "We Are Family," "Wash Day," "Nine Patch" blender row, "Rail Fence" blender row, "Nine Patch" blender row, "Twinkle," "Row Houses," and "Four Patch" blender row.

Both quilts pieced by Susan Ache; quilted by Maggi Honeyman

ABOVE: There's no reason a single row can't star in its own wall vignette. "Sand Pails" finishes out this summery tableaux, and the collected miniature sand-pail shovels look as if they could have been plucked right out of the appliqué row.

FACING PAGE: One nice thing about creating row quilts—there are no rules! That means you're not limited to using a row only once. Nor do you have to make your rows match the colors of the original design. Choose your favorite rows, decide on a combination of colors that suit your style, and you'll be "rowing" your way to quilt success in no time!

This quilt includes the following rows: "Twinkle," "Bitty Baskets," "X Row" blender row, "Bird on a Pumpkin," "X Row" blender row, "Bitty Baskets," "Twinkle," and "Flying Geese" blender row.

Pieced and quilted by Melissa Corey

Fall

Use a classic autumnal palette of deep browns, golds, greens, and reds for a row of falling foliage and acorns. A layered patchwork technique simplifies the piecing.

Designed by Lynne Hagmeier of Kansas Troubles Quilters

Finished row: 9" x 48"

Materials

Yardage is based on 42"-wide fabric.

½ yard of tan print for background
4" x 8" rectangle *each* of 8 assorted dark prints for Leaf blocks
4" x 8" rectangle *each* of 3 assorted medium-brown prints for Acorn blocks
4" x 8" rectangle *each* of 3 assorted dark-brown prints for blocks
Dark-green, dark-brown, and tan cotton thread
Size 12 dark-brown pearl cotton
Scrap of lightweight paper-backed fusible web
Size 10 embroidery needle

Cutting

All measurements include ¼"-wide seam allowances.

From the tan print, cut:
2 strips, 3½" x 42"; crosscut into 22 squares, 3½" x 3½"
1 strip, 2½" x 42"; crosscut into:
    3 rectangles, 2½" x 9½"
    2 rectangles, 2½" x 3½"
1 strip, 2" x 42"; crosscut into:
    2 rectangles, 2" x 6½"
    2 rectangles, 2" x 3½"
9 squares, 1⅝" x 1⅝"; cut in half diagonally to yield 18 triangles
2 rectangles, 1½" x 3½"

From the assorted dark prints, cut a *total* of:
15 squares, 3½" x 3½"; cut 6 *of the squares* in half diagonally to yield 12 triangles

From *each* of the 3 medium-brown print rectangles, cut:
2 squares, 3½" x 3½" (6 total)

From *each* of the 3 dark-brown print rectangles, cut:

1 square, 2½" x 2½" (3 total); cut in half diagonally to yield
  2 triangles (6 total)
2 rectangles, 2" x 3½"
9 squares, 1⅝" x 1⅝"; cut in half diagonally to yield 18 triangles
2 rectangles, 1½" x 3½"
Set aside the remainder for the leaf-stem appliqués.

Make the Leaf Blocks

1 With right sides up, layer an assorted dark triangle over a tan 3½" square, aligning the straight outer edges. Using dark-green thread, stitch approximately ⅛" from the triangle's raw diagonal edge. Repeat to make a total of 12 layered leaf-point squares.

Make 12.

2 Arrange four leaf-point squares, three assorted dark 3½" squares, and two tan 3½" squares in three horizontal rows as shown. Sew the pieces in each row together. Press the seam allowances as indicated. Sew the rows together. Press the seam allowances toward the middle row. Repeat to make a total of three Leaf blocks. The blocks should measure 9½" x 9½".

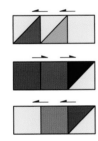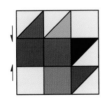

Make 3.

Make the Acorn Blocks

1 With right sides up, layer tan triangles over opposite corners of a medium-brown square, aligning the straight outer edges. Using tan thread, stitch ⅛" from the triangles' raw diagonal edges. Repeat to make a total of six layered acorn squares.

Make 6.

2 With right sides up, layer a dark-brown triangle over one of the remaining corners of each layered acorn square from step 1, aligning the straight edges. Using dark-brown thread, stitch ⅛" from the triangles' raw diagonal edges. Layer a tan triangle over the same

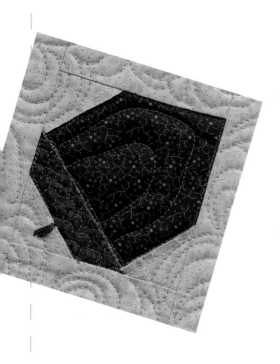

corner of each acorn square, aligning the straight edges. Using tan thread, stitch ⅛" from the triangles' long diagonal edges.

Make 6.

3 Lay out one tan 2" x 3½" rectangle, one acorn unit, and one tan 3½" square as shown. Lay out one acorn unit, one tan 2½" x 3½" rectangle, and one tan 1½" x 3½" rectangle as shown to create a vertical section. Lay out one acorn unit and one tan 3½" square as shown to create a second vertical section. Sew each section together; press the seam allowances toward the tan pieces. Place a 2" x 6½" rectangle between the vertical sections; sew together to create a row. Press the seam allowances toward the center rectangle. Sew the rows together. Press the seam allowances toward the top row. Repeat to make a total of two Acorn blocks that measure 9½" x 9½".

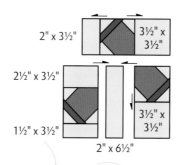

2" x 3½"
3½" x 3½"
2½" x 3½"
1½" x 3½"
3½" x 3½"
2" x 6½"

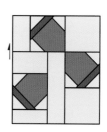

Make 2.

Assemble and Finish the Row

For additional information on appliqué and embroidery techniques, go to ShopMartingale.com/HowtoQuilt.

1 Arrange the blocks and three tan 2½" x 9½" rectangles as shown. Sew the pieces together, and press the seam allowances as indicated.

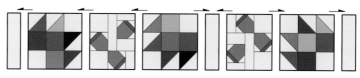

Row assembly

2 Using the pattern below, prepare the leaf stems for fusible-web appliqué. Referring to the photo on page 52 as needed, position the stems on the leaf blocks, extending them onto the adjacent background strip. Follow the manufacturer's instructions to fuse the shapes in place. Straight stitch around each stem and through the middle with matching brown thread to permanently attach the shapes to the background.

3 Using one strand of brown pearl cotton and the embroidery needle, make three to five straight stitches, placed close together, at the top of each acorn to make the acorn stems. Refer to the photo as needed.

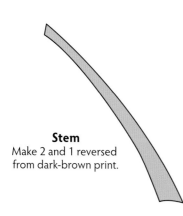

Stem
Make 2 and 1 reversed from dark-brown print.

Pattern is reversed for fusible appliqué and does not include seam allowance.

November

Designed by Lisa Bongean of Primitive Gatherings

Finished row: 10" x 48"

Materials

Yardage is based on 42"-wide fabric. Fat quarters are 18" x 21".

8½" x 10½" rectangle *each* of 6 assorted black prints for background
¼ yard of orange stripe for pumpkin appliqués
1 fat quarter of green print for vines
Scraps of assorted green prints for stem, leaf, bird, and star appliqués
Scraps of assorted purple prints for grape appliqués
Scrap of rust print for bird-wing appliqués
Size 12 pearl cotton in dark green, light green, and variegated gold
Size 11 straw needle for appliqué
Size 24 chenille needle for embroidery

Assemble and Appliqué the Row

For additional information on appliqué and embroidery techniques, go to ShopMartingale.com/HowtoQuilt.

1 Join the six black rectangles along the long edges in the desired order. Press the seam allowances open or in one direction.

2 Using the patterns at right and on pages 56 and 57, prepare the shapes for turned-edge appliqué. Make approximately 100" of bias stems and vines from the green fat quarter. Position the vines on the background strip and appliqué them in place. Position and appliqué the prepared shapes using the size 11 straw needle, referring to the photo above and the appliqué placement diagram on page 56 as needed.

3 Transfer the wing and small pumpkin detail lines to the shapes. Using the dark-green pearl cotton and the chenille needle, stem-stitch the small pumpkin detail lines. With light-green pearl cotton, blanket-stitch around the star and cross-stitch over the vines and stems. Using gold pearl cotton, stem-stitch the wing detail lines.

Blend rich prints in an appliquéd row that pays homage to November's dark and chilly nights. Add a touch of texture with hand-embroidered details.

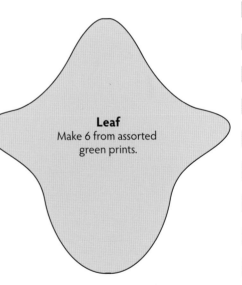

Leaf
Make 6 from assorted green prints.

Grape
Make 40 from assorted purple prints.

Patterns do not include seam allowances.

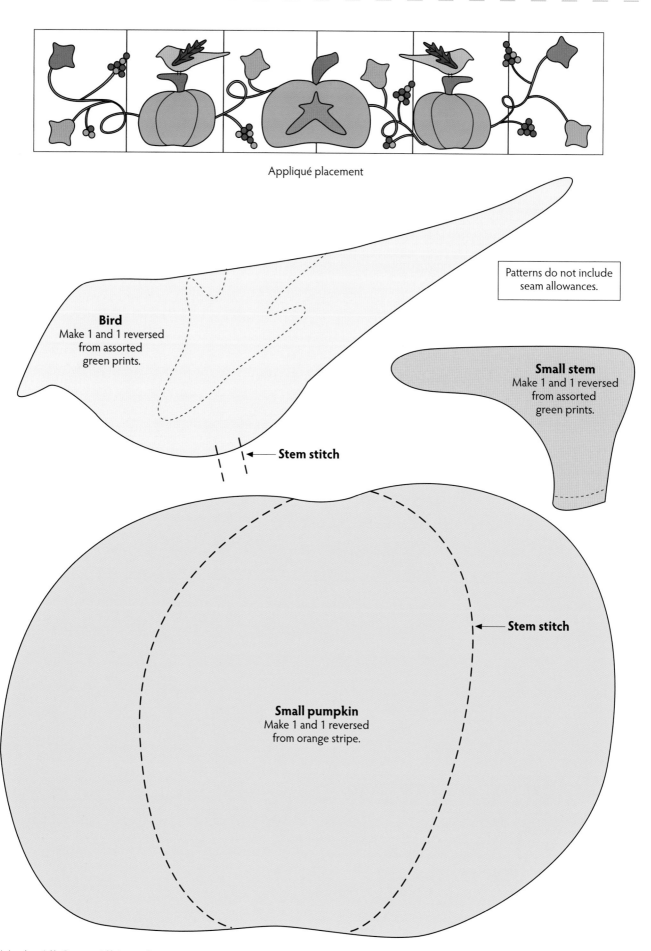

Appliqué placement

Patterns do not include
seam allowances.

Bird
Make 1 and 1 reversed
from assorted
green prints.

Small stem
Make 1 and 1 reversed
from assorted
green prints.

← **Stem stitch**

Small pumpkin
Make 1 and 1 reversed
from orange stripe.

← **Stem stitch**

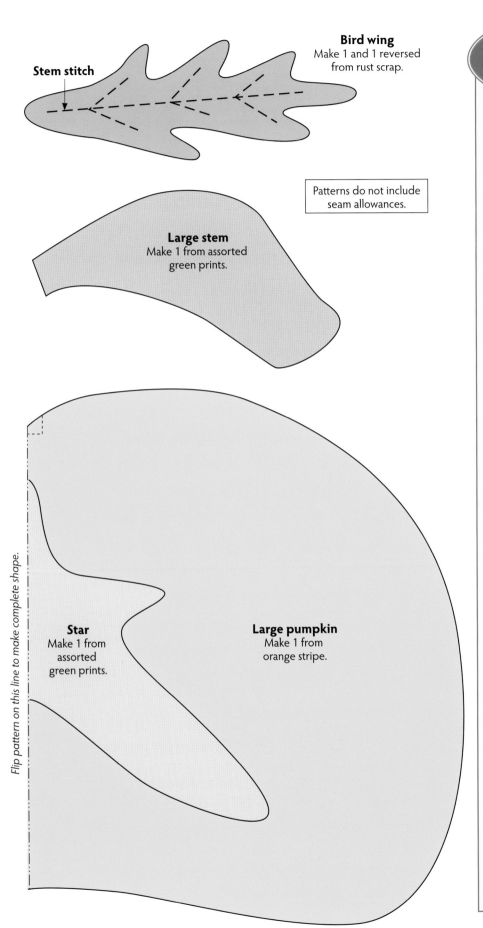

Bird wing
Make 1 and 1 reversed
from rust scrap.

Stem stitch

Patterns do not include
seam allowances.

Large stem
Make 1 from assorted
green prints.

Star
Make 1 from
assorted
green prints.

Large pumpkin
Make 1 from
orange stripe.

Flip pattern on this line to make complete shape.

As an owner of two quilt shop locations—one in Wisconsin and the other in California (primitivegatherings.us)—as well as being a fabric, pattern, and tool designer, Lisa is rarely found doing anything other than quilting.

- **I'm currently obsessed with** my new grandbaby, Jace.

- **If I'm not quilting, I'm** . . . I'm always quilting.

- **The best piece of advice (regarding quilting) I've received was** you don't have to follow a pattern.

- **My go-to snack food for a full day (or night) of quilting is** crunchy peanut butter on a spoon.

- **When I just can't get a quilt to come together,** I...sorry, I don't know what you're talking about. Mine always come together! LOL.

- **My go-to color combination is** scrappy.

- **I can't begin a new quilting project unless** I finish the current one. This is really the key to getting things done.

- **On my playlist while I'm quilting is** classic rock—Journey, Stevie Nicks, or *Investigation Discovery* on TV.

- **Beyond designing, my favorite part of making a quilt is** hand stitching wool or appliquéing cotton and wool.

- **One little tip that will make creating my row easier is** to do all the appliqués in wool instead of cotton. Needle-turn is not for everyone!

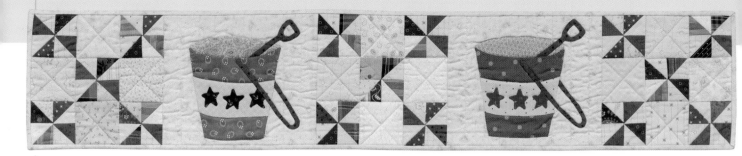

Sand Pails

Designed by Laurie Simpson of Minick and Simpson

Make a beachy-keen patchwork-and-appliqué row to celebrate summertime. For a patriotic look, use a combination of traditional red, white, and blue prints.

Finished row: 9" x 48"

Materials

Yardage is based on 42"-wide fabric. Fat eighths are 9" x 21".

¾ yard *total* of assorted cream prints for blocks and appliqués
¼ yard *total* of assorted blue prints for blocks and appliqués
⅛ yard *total* of assorted red prints for blocks and appliqués
1 fat eighth of blue print for sand-pail appliqués
1 fat eighth of red print for sand-pail appliqués

Cutting

All measurements include ¼"-wide seam allowances.

From the assorted cream prints, cut a *total* of:
2 squares, 11" x 11"
12 squares, 3½" x 3½"
31 squares, 2½" x 2½"

From the assorted blue prints, cut a *total* of:
17 squares, 2½" x 2½"

From the assorted red prints, cut a *total* of:
14 squares, 2½" x 2½"

Make the Pinwheel Blocks

1 Draw a diagonal line from corner to corner on the wrong side of each cream 2½" square. Layer a marked square over each blue and red 2½" square, right sides together. Sew ¼" from both sides of the marked lines. Cut the squares apart on the marked lines to make two half-square-triangle units from each pair (62 total). Press the seam allowances toward the blue and red. Square up each unit to 2" x 2".

Make 62 total.

2 Randomly select four half-square-triangle units and lay them out in two horizontal rows of two units each as shown. Sew the units in each row together. Press the seam allowances in opposite directions. Join the rows to make a pinwheel unit. Press the seam allowances in one direction. Repeat to make a total of 15 pinwheel units. You'll have two half-square-triangle units left over for another project.

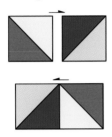
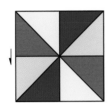

Make 15.

3 Lay out five pinwheel units and four cream 3½" squares in three horizontal rows. Sew the pieces in each row together. Press the seam allowances toward the squares. Join the rows to complete the block. Press the seam allowances toward the middle row. Make a total of three Pinwheel blocks; they should measure 9½" x 9½".

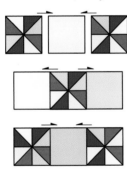
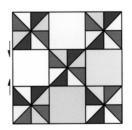

Make 3.

Make the Appliquéd Blocks

1 Using the patterns on pages 60 and 61, prepare the shapes for turned-edge appliqué. For more information on turned-edge appliqué, go to ShopMartingale.com/HowtoQuilt.

2 Using the photo on page 58 as a guide, center the sand-pail appliqués on the cream 11" background square and appliqué them in place. Make two blocks. Trim each block to 9½" x 9½".

Assemble the Row

Lay out the blocks side by side, alternating the Pinwheel blocks with the appliquéd blocks. Sew the blocks together. Press the seam allowances toward the appliquéd blocks.

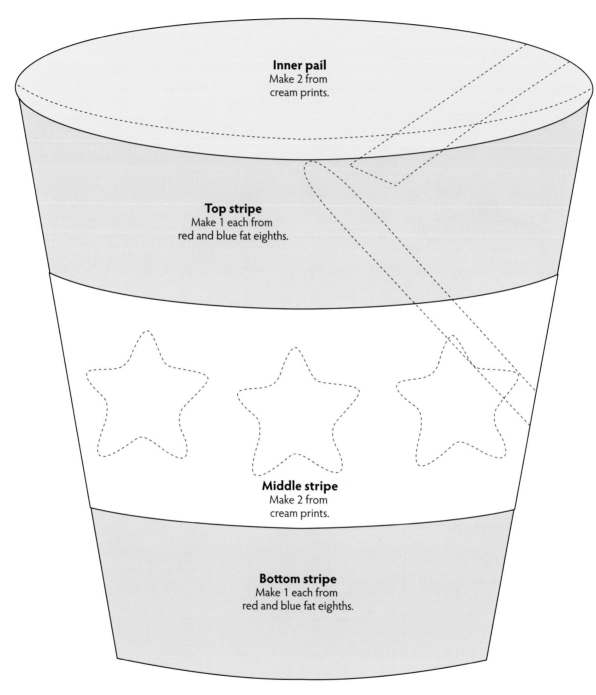

Inner pail
Make 2 from
cream prints.

Top stripe
Make 1 each from
red and blue fat eighths.

Middle stripe
Make 2 from
cream prints.

Bottom stripe
Make 1 each from
red and blue fat eighths.

Patterns do not include
seam allowances.

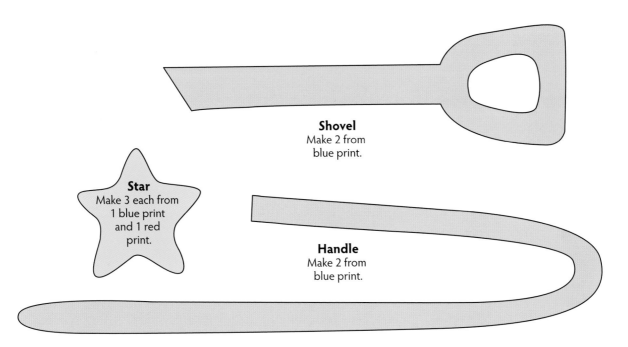

Shovel
Make 2 from
blue print.

Star
Make 3 each from
1 blue print
and 1 red
print.

Handle
Make 2 from
blue print.

Patterns do not include
seam allowances.

Appliqué placement

Birdies and Trees

Piece a festive holiday row that features a forest of fir trees interspersed with adorable appliquéd birds.

Designed by Corey Yoder of Little Miss Shabby

Finished row: 6" x 48"

Materials

Yardage is based on 42"-wide fabric.

½ yard of tan solid for background
⅛ yard of dark-brown print for tree trunks
⅛ yard *total* of 2 different green prints for treetops
5" x 5" square *each* of 7 assorted prints for bird appliqués
Scrap of dark-gray solid for bird-beak and leg appliqués
Scrap of red print for hat appliqué
Scrap of white print for hat-trim appliqué
¼ yard of 17"-wide lightweight paper-backed fusible web
7 buttons for birdie eyes, ⅛" diameter

Cutting

All measurements include ¼"-wide seam allowances.

From the tan solid, cut:
2 strips, 3½" x 42"; crosscut into:
    7 rectangles, 3½" x 6½"
    4 squares, 3½" x 3½"
    4 rectangles, 3" x 3½"
2 strips, 2" x 42"; crosscut into:
    2 rectangles, 2" x 6½"
    16 squares, 2" x 2"
1 strip, 1¾" x 42"; crosscut into 8 rectangles, 1¾" x 3½"

From the dark-brown print, cut:
2 rectangles, 1½" x 3½"
4 rectangles, 1" x 3½"

From the 2 green prints, cut a *total* of:
4 pairs of matching rectangles, 2" x 3½" (8 total)
2 rectangles, 3½" x 6½"

Make the Bird Strips

1 Using the patterns on page 64, prepare the shapes for fusible appliqué. For more information on fusible appliqué, go to ShopMartingale.com/HowtoQuilt. Position the prepared shapes on the seven tan 3½" x 6½" background rectangles, referring to the photo on page 62 as needed and being sure to keep the appliqués out of the seam allowances. Follow the manufacturer's instructions to fuse the shapes in place. Stitch around each appliqué using a zigzag or blanket stitch to permanently attach the shape to the background strip.

2 Stitch a button to each bird where indicated on the pattern.

Make the Tree Strips

1 Draw a diagonal line from corner to corner on the wrong side of each tan 2" square. Lay a marked square on one end of a green 2" x 3½" rectangle as shown, right sides together. Sew on the marked line. Trim ¼" from the stitching line. Press the seam allowances toward the corner. Lay another marked square on the opposite end of the rectangle as shown; stitch, trim, and press as before to make a small flying-geese unit. Repeat to make a total of eight units.

Make 8.

2 Sew tan 1¾" x 3½" rectangles to the sides of a dark-brown 1" x 3½" rectangle. Press the seam allowances toward the brown. Repeat to make a total of four tree-trunk units.

Make 4.

3 Sew two matching flying-geese units and one tree-trunk unit together as shown to make a skinny tree unit. Press the seam allowances toward the top of the unit. Repeat to make a total of four units.

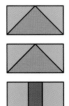 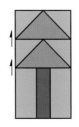

Make 4.

4 Repeat step 1 with the two green 3½" x 6½" rectangles and the four tan 3½" squares to make two large flying-geese units.

5 Sew tan 3" x 3½" rectangles to the sides of each dark-brown 1½" x 3½" rectangle to make two wide tree-trunk units. Press the seam allowances toward the dark brown.

6 Sew a large flying-geese unit to a wide tree-trunk unit as shown to make a wide tree unit. Press the seam allowances toward the flying-geese unit. Repeat to make a total of two units.

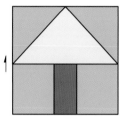

Make 2.

Assemble the Row

Refer to the row assembly diagram below to join the appliquéd bird strips, the skinny and wide tree units, and the tan 2" x 6½" rectangles as shown to complete the row. Press the seam allowances open.

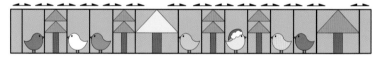

Row assembly

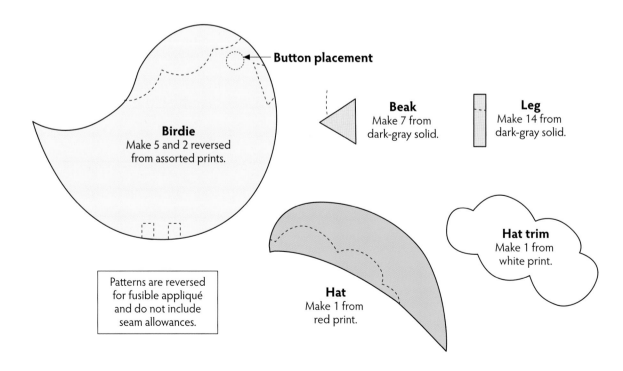

Birdie
Make 5 and 2 reversed
from assorted prints.

← **Button placement**

Beak
Make 7 from
dark-gray solid.

Leg
Make 14 from
dark-gray solid.

Hat trim
Make 1 from
white print.

Hat
Make 1 from
red print.

Patterns are reversed
for fusible appliqué
and do not include
seam allowances.

Bunny Playdate

Designed by Janet Clare

Finished row: 9" x 48"

Bunnies frolic and chase butterflies across a row that's perfect for springtime decor or an Easter quilt.

Materials

Yardage is based on 42"-wide fabric.

½ yard of cream print for background
⅓ yard of taupe print for bunny appliqués
5" x 5" square of blue print for butterfly appliqués
8" x 8" square of lightweight cardstock
½ yard of 17"-wide lightweight paper-backed fusible web
4 small brads, ⅛" diameter
Dark-gray embroidery floss
Size 26 hand-embroidery needle

Cutting

All measurements include ¼"-wide seam allowances.

From the cream print, cut:
4 rectangles, 9½" x 12½"

Assemble and Appliqué the Row

1 Trace the bunny body, leg, ear, and tail shapes (patterns are on page 67) onto cardstock. Transfer the dots to each piece. Cut out the shapes. Carefully push a pin through the marked dots on each piece to make a neat hole.

2 Place the legs, ears, and tail in the correct positions on the body, placing one ear and one leg behind the body. With the holes aligned, join the pieces by pushing a brad through the holes as shown on page 66. You now have a jointed template.

In addition to designing fabric and patterns, Janet is a full-time mother to two boys. "I try to find joy in the mundane, and don't believe in keeping things 'for best,'" Janet says from her home in England (janetclare.co.uk).

- **I'm currently obsessed with** cross-stitch samplers.

- **If I'm not quilting, I'm** thinking about quilting.

- **The best piece of advice (regarding quilting) I've received was** never, ever point out your mistakes.

- **My go-to snack food for a full day (or night) of quilting is** toast and butter.

- **When I just can't get a quilt to come together,** I take my beloved dog, Betty, for a walk.

- **My go-to color combination is** cream and indigo.

- **I can't begin a new quilting project unless** I have a title and a new sketchbook ready.

- **On my playlist while I'm quilting is** BBC Radio 4 (news, current affairs).

- **Beyond designing, my favorite part of making a quilt is** finishing it.

- **One little tip that will make creating my row easier is** to use small brass brads to attach the cardstock bunny legs to the cardstock bunny body. The legs will swivel so you can adjust the positions as you wish. That way, no two bunnies need be identical as they frolic across the row.

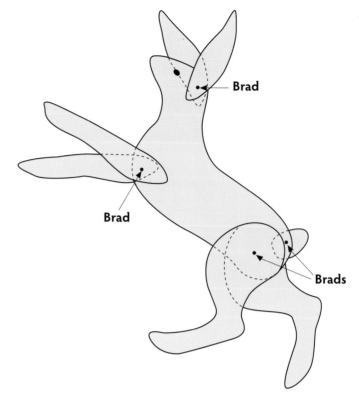

Join legs, ears, and tail to body with brads to make an adjustable appliqué pattern.

3 Referring to the photo on page 65 as a guide, arrange the rabbit template in the desired position. Lay the template on the paper side of the fusible web and trace around it. Rearrange the rabbit and make three additional tracings, leaving at least ½" of space around each one. Trace the butterfly pattern on page 67 onto the fusible web four times. Roughly cut out each shape, remove the paper backings, and fuse the pieces to the wrong side of the appropriate fabrics. Cut out each shape on the marked lines. For more information on fusible appliqué, go to ShopMartingale.com/HowtoQuilt.

4 Position the prepared shapes on the cream background rectangles. Follow the manufacturer's instructions to fuse the shapes in place. Using a contrasting thread, free-motion stitch around each shape, adding details as you go. For a tutorial on Janet's machine-drawing technique, visit her website at janetclare.co.uk.

5 With two strands of gray floss and the embroidery needle, satin stitch the eye and nose details. For more information on working the stitch, go to ShopMartingale.com/HowtoQuilt.

6 Sew the appliquéd rectangles together side by side along the short edges.

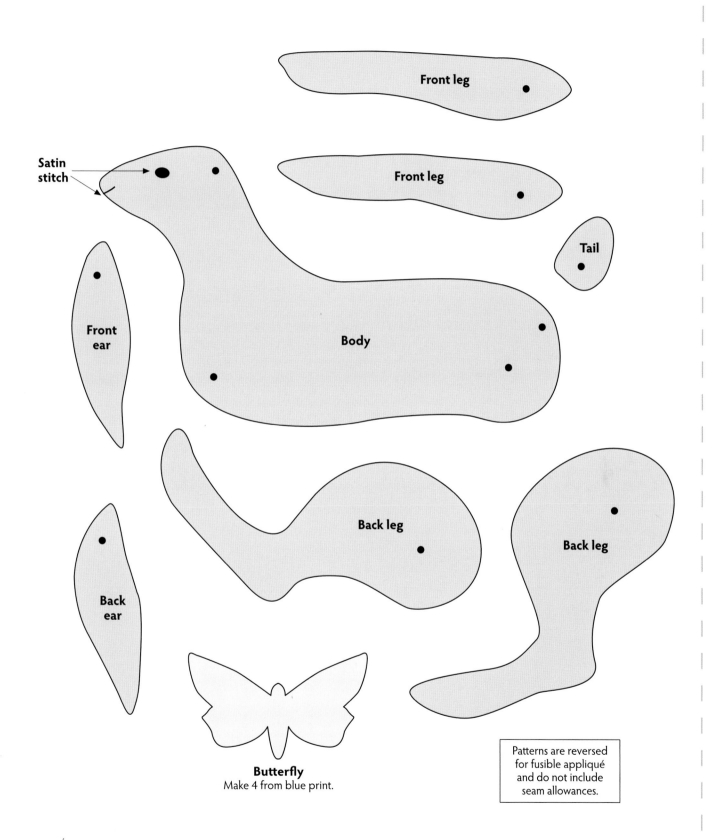

Front leg

Front leg

Satin stitch

Tail

Front ear

Body

Back leg

Back leg

Back ear

Butterfly
Make 4 from blue print.

Patterns are reversed
for fusible appliqué
and do not include
seam allowances.

Pretty pastel Double
Nine Patch blocks frame
a striking center appliqué
of intertwining vines in a
row that brings to mind
spring in full bloom.

Garland Knot

Designed by Brenda Riddle of Acorn Quilt and Gift Company

Finished row: 9" x 48"

Materials

Yardage is based on 42"-wide fabric. Fat quarters are 18" x 21".

½ yard of off-white solid for background

¼ yard of light-blue lattice print for blocks and appliqué background

1 fat quarter of light-green print for vine and leaf appliqués

6" x 6" square _each_ of 5 assorted green prints for leaf appliqués

5" x 5" square of pink print for berry appliqués

¾ yard of 17"-wide lightweight paper-backed fusible web

Cutting

All measurements include ¼"-wide seam allowances.

From the off-white solid, cut:

1 strip, 3½" x 42"; crosscut into 8 squares, 3½" x 3½"

4 strips, 1½" x 42"; crosscut into:

    1 strip, 1½" x 32"

    2 strips, 1½" x 31"

    2 strips, 1½" x 16"

1 strip, 5½" x 31"

From the light-blue lattice print, cut:

5 strips, 1½" x 42"; crosscut into:

    2 strips, 1½" x 32"

    2 strips, 1½" x 31"

    1 strip, 1½" x 16"

From the fusible web, cut:

1 strip, 1" x 24"

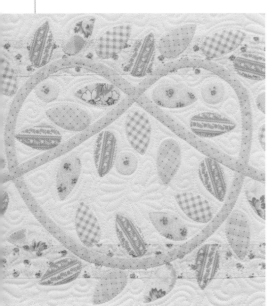

Make the Double Nine Patch Blocks

1 Sew light-blue 1½" x 32" strips to both long edges of the off-white 1½" x 32" strip to make strip set A. Press the seam allowances toward the blue. Crosscut the strip set into 20 segments, 1½" wide.

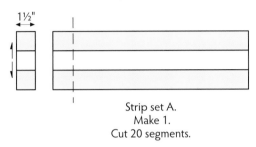

Strip set A.
Make 1.
Cut 20 segments.

2 Sew off-white 1½" x 16" strips to both long edges of the light-blue 1½" x 16" strip to make strip set B. Press the seam allowances toward the blue. Crosscut the strip set into 10 segments, 1½" wide.

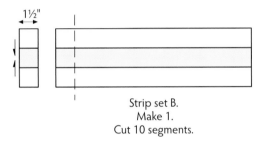

Strip set B.
Make 1.
Cut 10 segments.

3 Join A segments to opposite sides of a B segment to make a nine-patch unit. Repeat to make a total of 10 units.

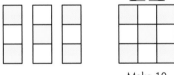

Make 10.

4 Arrange five nine-patch units and four off-white 3½" squares into three horizontal rows as shown. Sew the pieces in each row together. Press the seam allowances toward the off-white squares. Join the rows. Press the seam allowances open. Repeat to make two blocks. The blocks should measure 9½" x 9½".

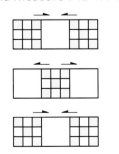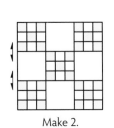

Make 2.

Make the Appliquéd Strip

1 Sew each light-blue 1½" x 31" strip to an off-white 1½" x 31" strip along the long edges. Press the seam allowances toward the blue.

Make 2.

2 Join the strips from step 1 to the long edges of the off-white 5½" x 31" strip. Press the seam allowances toward the step 1 strips.

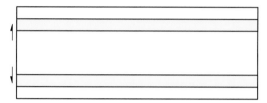

3 To make the bias strips for the vine, fold over the top-left corner of the light-green fat quarter as shown and press the fold. Unfold the fat quarter, lay your ruler on the fold, and cut along the fold line. Measuring from the first cut, cut a 1"-wide bias strip from the bottom part of the fat quarter. Follow the manufacturer's instructions to apply the fusible-web 1" x 24" strip to the wrong side of the bias strip. Trim away any excess fabric from the ends of the strip that are not backed with fusible web. From this strip, cut three ¼"-wide strips. You'll need approximately 57" of fusible bias strip for the vine.

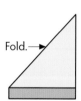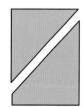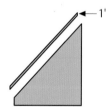

Fold. →   ← 1"

4 Using the patterns at left, prepare the shapes for fusible appliqué. For more information, go to ShopMartingale.com/HowtoQuilt. Position the prepared vine, leaf, and berry shapes on the pieced background strip, referring to the photo on page 68. Follow the manufacturer's instructions to fuse the shapes in place. Stitch around each appliqué using a zigzag stitch, blanket stitch, or the stitch of your choice to permanently attach the shapes to the background strip. Trim the strip to 9½" x 30½", keeping the appliqué design centered.

Assemble the Row

Sew a Double Nine Patch block to each end of the appliquéd strip. Press the seam allowances open.

Leaf
Make 60 from light-green
print and assorted
green prints.

Berry
Make 9 from
pink print.

Patterns do not include
seam allowances.

Winter Friends

Designed by Kathy Schmitz of Kathy Schmitz Studio

A delightful redwork winter scene of a friendly snowman is the star of this row. Carry through the color scheme with simple red-and-cream patchwork blocks.

Finished row: 8" x 48"

Materials

Yardage is based on 42"-wide fabric.

⅝ yard of cream print for blocks and pieced units
⅜ yard *total* of 4 assorted red prints for blocks and pieced units
Water-soluble fabric marker or red fine-point permanent marker
Red embroidery floss
Size 26 hand-embroidery needle

Cutting

All measurements include ¼"-wide seam allowances.

From the cream print, cut:

1 strip, 3" x 42"; crosscut into 10 squares, 3" x 3"
2 strips, 2½" x 42"; crosscut into 24 squares, 2½" x 2½"
1 rectangle, 10" x 12"
4 squares, 5¼" x 5¼"

From the 4 assorted red prints, cut a *total* of:

3 squares, 4½" x 4½"
26 squares, 3" x 3"

Make the Embroidered Block

1 Trace the pattern on page 75 onto the right side of the cream 10" x 12" rectangle using the fabric marker or red pen.

2 Using two strands of red floss and the embroidery needle, stitch the design, working the solid lines with a stem stitch, the dashed lines with a running stitch, and the dots with a French knot. For more information on embroidery stitches, go to ShopMartingale.com/HowtoQuilt.

3 Square up the stitched piece to 8½" x 10½", keeping the design centered.

Make the Patchwork Units

1 Draw a diagonal line from corner to corner on the wrong side of the 10 cream 3" squares. Layer a marked square on top of an assorted red 3" square, right sides together. Stitch ¼" from both sides of the marked lines. Cut the squares apart on the marked line to make two half-square-triangle units. Repeat with the remaining marked squares to make a total of 20 units. Press the seam allowances open. Square up each unit to 2½" x 2½".

Make 20.

2 Sew the half-square-triangle units together as shown to make a total of five rows. Press the seam allowances open.

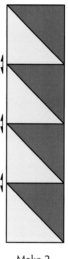

Make 2.   Make 3.

3 Place two assorted red 3" squares on a cream 5¼" square, right sides together with the red squares overlapping at the center. Draw a line from corner to corner through the red squares. Stitch ¼" from both sides of the marked line. Cut the layered squares apart on the marked line. Press the seam allowances open.

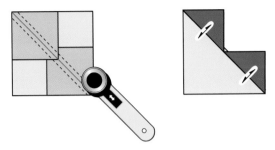

4 Position a red 3" square on the cream triangle of a unit from step 3 as shown, right sides together. Draw a line from corner to corner on the red square as shown. Stitch ¼" from each side of the marked line. Cut on the marked line to make two flying-geese units. Press the seam allowances open. Repeat with the remaining unit from step 3 to make a total of four flying-geese units. Square up each unit to 2½" x 4½".

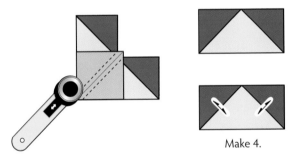

Make 4.

5 Repeat steps 3 and 4 to make a total of 16 flying-geese units.

6 Join four flying-geese units along the long edges as shown to make a row. Press the seam allowances open. Set aside the 12 remaining flying-geese units for the Star blocks.

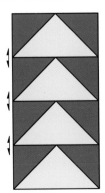

Make the Star Blocks

1 Draw a diagonal line from corner to corner on the wrong side of 12 cream 2½" squares. Place marked squares on opposite corners of a red 4½" square, right sides together. Sew on the marked lines. Trim ¼" from the stitching lines. Press the seam allowances open. Sew cream squares to the opposite corners to make a square-in-a-square unit. Repeat to make a total of three units.

Make 3.

2 Lay out one square-in-a-square unit, four flying-geese units, and four cream 2½" squares in three horizontal rows as shown. Sew the pieces in each row together. Press the seam allowances open. Join the rows. Press the seam allowances open. Repeat to make a total of three blocks.

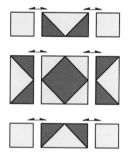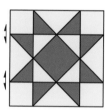

Make 3.

Assemble the Row

Arrange the embroidered block, the half-square-triangle rows, the flying-geese row, and the Star blocks as shown. Sew the pieces together. Press the seam allowances open.

Row assembly

Alternating flower appliqués and scrappy patchwork blocks infuse this row with a touch of romance.

He Loves Me...

Designed by Kate Spain

Finished row: 6" x 48"

Materials

Yardage is based on 42"-wide fabric. Fat eighths are 9" x 21".

⅜ yard *total* of assorted bright prints for blocks and flower appliqués
¼ yard of white solid for appliquéd blocks
1 fat eighth of green solid for stem and leaf appliqués
⅛ yard of 17"-wide lightweight paper-backed fusible web

Cutting

All measurements include ¼"-wide seam allowances.

From the assorted bright prints, cut
48 squares, 2" x 2"
From the white solid, cut a *total* of:
5 squares, 6½" x 6½"

Make the Blocks

1 To make the pieced blocks, randomly select 12 bright 2" squares and arrange them in four rows of three squares each. Sew the squares in each row together. Press the seam allowances in opposite directions from row to row. Join the rows. Press the seam allowances in one direction. Repeat to make a total of four blocks.

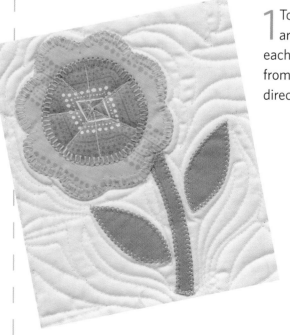

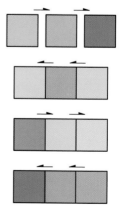

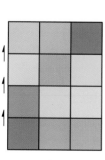

Make 4.

2 To make the appliquéd blocks, use the patterns below to prepare the shapes for fusible appliqué. For more information on fusible appliqué, go to ShopMartingale.com/HowtoQuilt. Referring to the photo on page 76 as needed, center one flower petal, one flower center, two leaves, and one stem on each white 6½" square. Follow the manufacturer's instructions to fuse the shapes in place. Stitch around each appliqué using a zigzag stitch, blanket stitch, or the stitch of your choice to permanently attach the shape to the background strip.

Assemble the Row

Alternately arrange the pieced and appliquéd blocks into a horizontal row. Sew the blocks together. Press the seam allowances toward the pieced blocks.

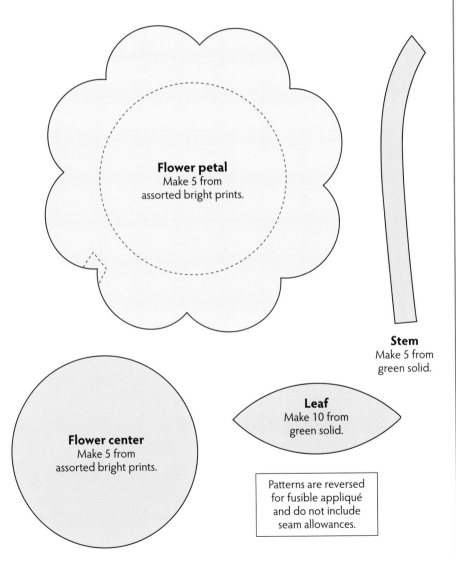

Flower petal
Make 5 from
assorted bright prints.

Stem
Make 5 from
green solid.

Flower center
Make 5 from
assorted bright prints.

Leaf
Make 10 from
green solid.

Patterns are reversed
for fusible appliqué
and do not include
seam allowances.

HERE'S THE
Skinny
FROM KATE SPAIN

Kate Spain is a Rhode Island School of Design–trained artist who licenses her nature-inspired drawings, patterns, and photographs. As part of her design work, Kate creates fabric lines in vivid, harmonious color palettes. Visit her online shop at ShopKateSpain.com.

- **I'm currently obsessed with** mini quilting templates.

- **If I'm not quilting, I'm** drawing or playing with our three cats.

- **The best piece of advice (regarding quilting) I've received was** to read a quilt pattern all the way through before starting to cut any fabric.

- **My go-to snack food for a full day (or night) of quilting is** any kind of nut.

- **When I just can't get a quilt to come together,** I pick up scraps and sew them together, improv-style. This helps me get back in the flow.

- **My go-to color combination is** blue and green.

- **I can't begin a new quilting project unless** I clean up from the last quilting project. If it doesn't start clean, I'd be buried under fabric when finished.

- **On my playlist while I'm quilting is** anything by ABBA.

- **Beyond designing, my favorite part of making a quilt is** free-motion quilting. It's like doodling with thread.

- **One little tip that will make creating my row better is** to fussy cut a print for the center of each flower to create interest.

Meadow Rose

Designed by Jen Kingwell

Grow a garden
of patchwork flowers
from colorful fabrics.
Display each one in its
own charming basket
made from black and
white prints.

Finished row: 8" x 48"

Materials

Yardage is based on 42"-wide fabric.

½ yard *total* of assorted bright prints for flower petals, centers, stems, and leaves

½ yard *total* of assorted light prints for flower backgrounds and baskets

¼ yard *total* of assorted black prints for baskets

Template plastic

Cutting

All measurements include ¼"-wide seam allowances. Trace patterns A–H on page 83 onto template plastic and cut them out. Use the templates to cut the flower pieces from the fabrics indicated below.

Cutting is for one block. Select one light print for the flower background, a different light print for the basket, one bright print for the flower, a different bright print for the stem and leaves, and a third bright print for the flower center (optional; the photo shows some flowers with centers and some without).

FOR EACH BLOCK (REPEAT 8 TIMES)

From one light print, cut:

2 rectangles, 1½" x 6½"

1 A and 1 A reversed piece

1 C and 1 C reversed piece

1 E and 1 E reversed piece

1F and 1 F reversed piece

From a different light print, cut:

1 square, 3¼" x 3¼"; cut into quarters diagonally to yield 4 triangles (you'll use 1 and have 3 left over)

1 square, 2⅞" x 2⅞"; cut in half diagonally to yield 2 triangles

1 square, 2⅜" x 2⅜"

From one bright print, cut:

5 B pieces

From a different bright print, cut:

1 D and 1 D reversed piece

1 G piece

From a third bright print, cut:

1 H piece (optional)

From one black print, cut:

1 square, 3¼" x 3¼"; cut into quarters diagonally to yield 4 triangles
(you'll use 3 and have 1 left over)

1 square, 2⅜" x 2⅜"

Make the Blocks

Use the pieces cut for one block.

1 Sew the B pieces together along the straight edges as shown to make a flower-petal unit. Press the seam allowances in one direction.

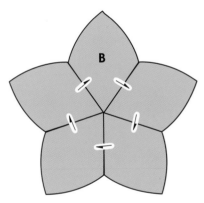

2 Stitch the A and A reversed pieces to the top of the flower-petal unit. Press the seam allowances toward the A pieces.

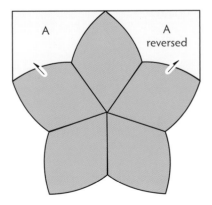

3 Stitch the C and C reversed pieces to the sides of the flower-petal unit. Press the seam allowances toward the C pieces.

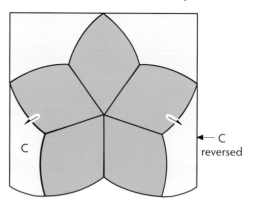

4 Join the E and F pieces to the D piece as shown. Press the seam allowances toward the E and F pieces. Repeat with the E, F, and D reversed pieces to make the leaf units.

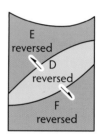

5 Sew the G piece between the leaf units from step 4. Press the seam allowances toward the G piece.

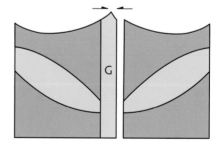

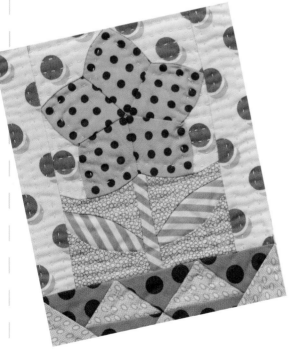

6 Join the flower unit to the stem/leaf unit. Press the seam allowances toward the flower unit. If desired, center the H piece on the flower and appliqué it in place using your favorite method. For more information on appliqué methods, go to ShopMartingale.com/HowtoQuilt.

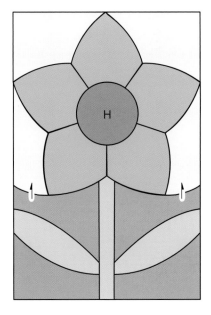

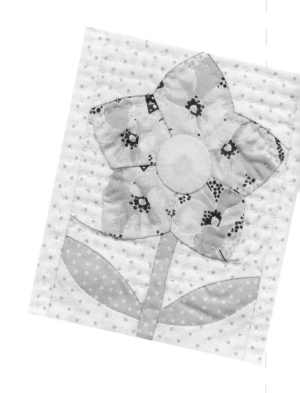

7 Add the light 1½" x 6½" rectangles to the sides of the unit. Press the seam allowances toward the rectangles.

8 To make the basket unit, draw a diagonal line from corner to corner on the wrong side of the light 2⅜" square. Layer the marked square on top of the black 2⅜" square, right sides together. Stitch ¼" from each side of the marked line. Cut the squares apart on the marked line to make two half-square-triangle units. Press the seam allowances toward the black.

Make 2.

9 Sew the small black and light quarter-square triangles to the half-square-triangle units as shown. Press the seam allowances in the direction indicated.

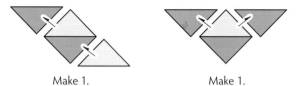

Make 1.   Make 1.

10 Sew the step 9 units together, and then add the large light half-square triangles. Press the seam allowances as indicated.

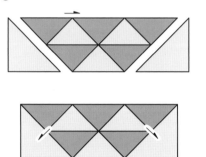

11 Join the basket unit to the bottom of the flower unit. Press the seam allowances open.

12 Repeat steps 1–11 to make a total of eight blocks.

Assemble the Row

Lay out the blocks side by side in one horizontal row. Sew the blocks together. Press the seam allowances open.

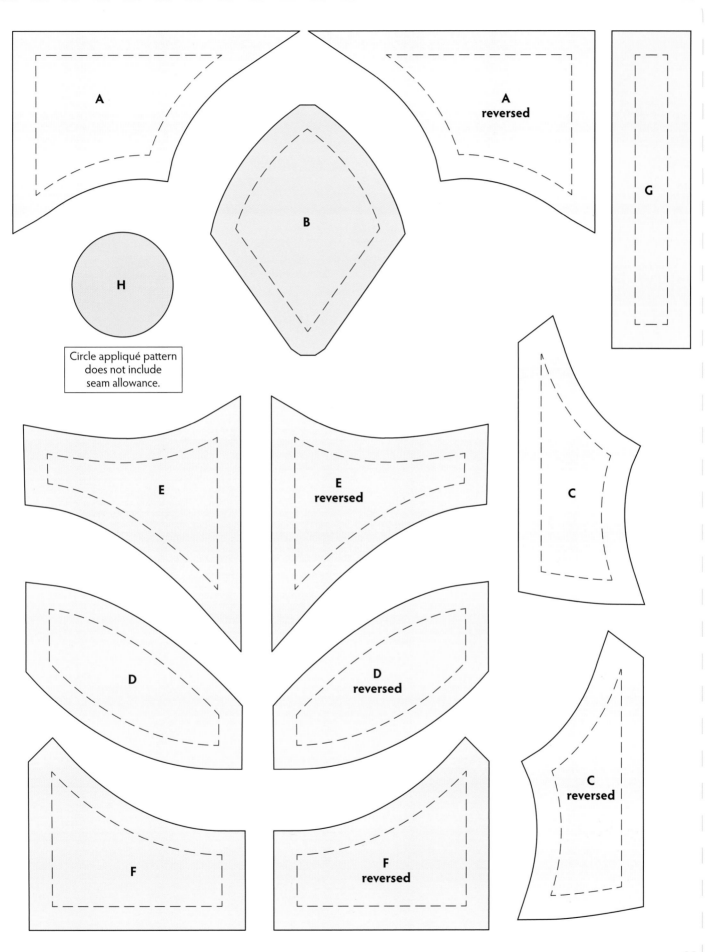

Circle appliqué pattern
does not include
seam allowance.

Twinkle

Designed by Camille Roskelley of Thimble Blossoms

Stunning graphic stars glitter across this jubilant row that comes together quickly from flying-geese and half-square-triangle units.

Finished row: 9" x 48"

Materials

Yardage is based on 42"-wide fabric. Fat eighths are 9" x 21".

1 fat eighth *each* of 4 assorted fabrics for block backgrounds
9" x 9" square *each* of 4 assorted fabrics for block outer-star point
7" x 7" square *each* of 4 assorted fabrics for block inner-star points
⅛ yard of white solid for sashing
8" x 8" square of green print for sashing
2" x 2" square *each* of 4 assorted prints for block centers

Cutting

All measurements include"-wide seam allowances.

From *each* of the 4 background fabrics, cut:
4 squares, 2⅜" x 2⅜" (16 total)
4 rectangles, 2" x 3½" (16 total)
8 squares, 2" x 2" (32 total)
From *each* of the 4 inner-star-point fabrics, cut:
8 squares, 2" x 2" (32 total)
From *each* of the 4 outer-star-point fabrics, cut:
4 squares, 2⅜" x 2⅜" (16 total)
4 rectangles, 2" x 3½" (16 total)
From the white solid, cut:
6 squares, 3½" x 3½"
4 rectangles, 2" x 3½"
From the green print, cut:
3 squares, 3½" x 3½"
2 rectangles, 2" x 3½"

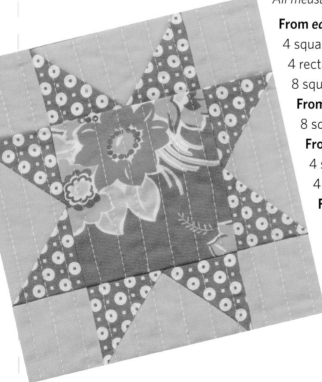

Make the Star Blocks

1 Select one block-center 2" square and the pieces from one background fabric, one inner-star-point fabric, and one outer-star-point fabric.

2 Draw a diagonal line from corner to corner on the wrong side of each outer-star-point 2⅜" square. Layer a marked square on top of each background 2⅜" square, right sides together. Stitch ¼" from each side of the marked lines. Cut the squares apart on the marked lines to make two half-square-triangle units from each pair (eight total). Press the seam allowances toward the darker fabric.

Make 8.

3 Lay out two half-square-triangle units and two background 2" squares in two horizontal rows as shown. Sew the pieces in each row together. Press the seam allowances toward the background squares. Join the rows. Press the seam allowances open. Repeat to make a total of four corner units.

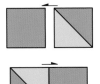

Make 4.

4 Draw a diagonal line from corner to corner on the wrong side of each inner-star-point 2" square. Lay a marked square on one end of a background 2" x 3½" rectangle as shown, right sides together. Sew on the marked line. Trim ¼" from the stitching line. Press the seam allowances toward the corner. Lay another marked square on the opposite end of the rectangle as shown; stitch, trim, and press as before to make a flying-geese unit. Repeat to make a total of four units.

 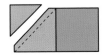

Make 4.

5 Sew each flying-geese unit to an outer-star-point 2" x 3½" rectangle along the long edges to make a side unit.

Make 4.

6 Lay out the corner units, the side units, and a center square in three horizontal rows. Sew the pieces in each row together. Press the seam allowances toward the side units. Join the rows and press the seam allowances toward the top and bottom rows.

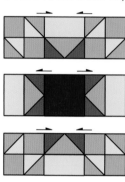 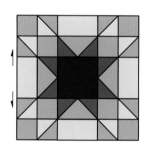

7 Repeat steps 1–6 to make a total of four blocks.

Assemble the Row

1 Sew white 3½" squares to the top and bottom of a green 3½" square. Press the seam allowances toward the green. Repeat to make a total of three wide sashing units. Sew white 2" x 3½" rectangles to the top and bottom of a green 2" x 3½" rectangle. Press the seam allowances toward the green. Repeat to make a total of two narrow sashing units.

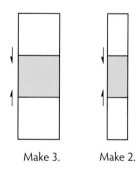

Make 3.   Make 2.

2 Alternately arrange the blocks and wide sashing units into one horizontal row. Add the narrow sashing units to the ends of the row, referring to the photo on page 84. Sew the pieces together. Press the seam allowances toward the sashing units.

Bitty Baskets

Designed by Betsy Chutchian of Betsy's Best Quilts and More

Finished row: 8" x 48"

Materials

Yardage is based on 42"-wide fabric. Fat quarters are 18" x 21".

½ yard *total* of 3 tan prints for blocks

½ yard *total* of 2 indigo and 2 brown prints for blocks and appliqués

1 fat quarter of cream print for blocks

Cutting

All measurements include ¼"-wide seam allowances. Label the triangles as you cut them to make piecing easier.

From the cream print, cut:

2 squares, 6⅝" x 6⅝"

1 square, 5¼" x 5¼"; cut into quarters diagonally to yield
    4 triangles (A)

From the tan prints, cut a *total* of:

2 matching squares, 5¼" x 5¼"; cut into quarters diagonally to
    yield 8 triangles (A)

4 matching squares, 5" x 5"; cut in half diagonally to yield
    8 triangles (B)

4 squares, 4½" x 4½"

**From the remainder of the cream print and tan prints,
    cut a *total* of:**

30 squares, 1⅞" x 1⅞"; cut in half diagonally to yield 60 triangles (C)

From the indigo and brown prints, cut a *total* of:

3 squares, 4½" x 4½"

3 pairs of matching squares, 2⅞" x 2⅞"; cut in half diagonally to yield
    12 triangles (D)

42 squares, 1⅞" x 1⅞"; cut in half diagonally to yield 84 triangles (C)

Baskets large and small are interspersed with traditional pieced Duck and Ducklings blocks. This block is also known as Pine Burr, but the image of baby ducklings is so much sweeter!

Make the Appliquéd Blocks

1 Using the patterns on page 90, prepare the shapes for turned-edge appliqué. For more information on turned-edge appliqué, go to ShopMartingale.com/HowtoQuilt.

2 Center a large basket shape on a cream 6⅝" square that has been turned on point; appliqué it in place. Trim the square to 6⅛" x 6⅛". Sew matching tan B triangles to opposite sides of the square. Press the seam allowances toward the triangles. Repeat on the opposite sides of the square. Repeat to make a total of two large Basket blocks. Square up each block to 8½" x 8½", keeping the appliqué centered.

Make 2.

3 Center a small basket shape on a tan 4½" square and appliqué it in place. Repeat to make a total of four small Basket blocks.

Make 4.

Make the Pieced Blocks

1 Using four matching tan or cream A triangles, sew a triangle to opposite corners of an indigo or brown 4½" square. Press the seam allowances toward the triangles. Repeat on the opposite sides of the square. Repeat to make a total of three units.

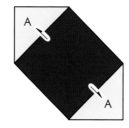 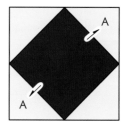

Make 3.

2 Sew a cream or tan C triangle to an indigo or brown C triangle along the long edges to make a half-square-triangle unit. Press the seam allowances toward the darker triangle. Repeat to make a total of 60 units. You'll use the remaining 24 indigo or brown C triangles in the next step.

Make 60.

3 Randomly select three half-square-triangle units and one indigo or brown C triangle and sew them together as shown. Press the seam allowances away from the triangle. Repeat to make a total of 12 long units. In the same manner, join two half-square-triangle units and one indigo or brown C triangle as shown. Repeat to make a total of 12 short units.

Make 12 of each.

4 Sew one long unit and one short unit from step 3 to adjacent sides of an indigo or brown D triangle. Press the seam allowances toward the D triangle. Repeat to make a total of 12 corner units.

Make 12.

5 Using four corner units with matching indigo or brown D triangles, sew the units to opposite sides of a step 1 unit. Press the seam allowances open. Repeat on the remaining two sides. Repeat to make a total of three pieced blocks.

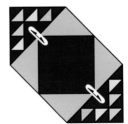

Make 3.

Assemble the Row

1 Sew two small appliquéd Basket blocks together to make a vertical row. Press the seam allowances open. Repeat to make a total of two rows.

2 Referring to the photo on page 87 as needed, alternately arrange the pieced blocks and large Basket blocks side by side in one horizontal row, placing the pieced block with the cream inner triangles in the center. Sew the blocks together. Add the small basket rows from step 1 to the ends of the row. Press the seam allowances open.

Make 2.

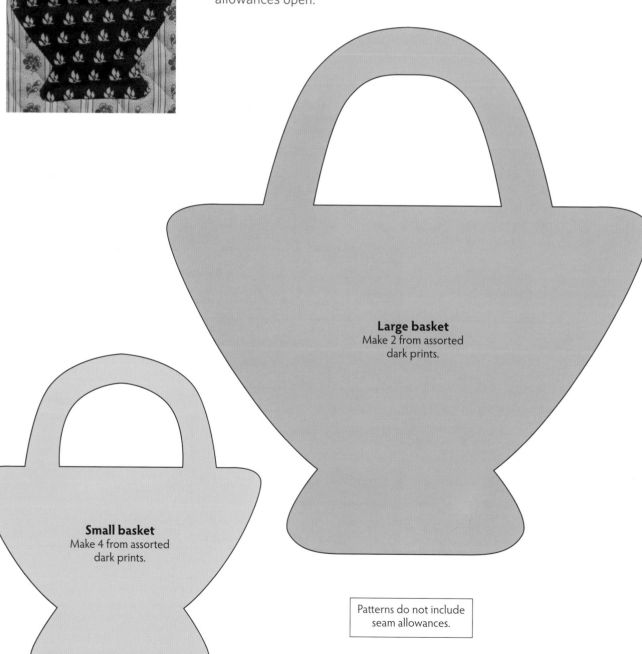

Large basket
Make 2 from assorted dark prints.

Small basket
Make 4 from assorted dark prints.

Patterns do not include seam allowances.

Double Stars

Designed by Barbara Brackman

Finished row: 8" x 48"

Materials

Yardage is based on 42"-wide fabric.

½ yard *total* of assorted light-tan prints for outer-star points

¼ yard of tan-and-red print for inner-star background

¼ yard *total* of assorted dark prints for outer-star points

⅛ yard *total* of assorted red prints for inner-star points

6" x 8" rectangle of red print for block centers

Six Double Star blocks make for a graphic and eye-catching row. Add harmony to the scrappy look by choosing one fabric to use for all of the star centers.

Cutting

All measurements include ¼"-wide seam allowances.

From the assorted red prints, cut a *total* of:
48 squares, 1½" x 1½"

From the tan-and-red print, cut:
3 strips, 1½" x 42"; crosscut into:
    24 rectangles, 1½" x 2½"
    24 squares, 1½" x 1½"

From the red rectangle, cut:
6 squares, 2½" x 2½"

From the assorted dark prints, cut a *total* of:
48 squares, 2½" x 2½"

From the assorted light-tan prints, cut a *total* of:
24 rectangles, 2½" x 4½"
24 squares, 2½" x 2½"

Make the Double Star Blocks

1 Draw a diagonal line from corner to corner on the wrong side of each assorted red 1½" square. Lay a marked square on one end of a tan-and-red print 1½" x 2½" rectangle as shown on page 92, right sides together. Sew on the marked line. Trim ¼" from the stitching line. Press the seam allowances toward the corner. Lay another marked square on the opposite

end of the rectangle as shown; stitch, trim, and press as before to make a small flying-geese unit. Repeat to make a total of 24 units.

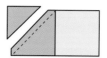

Make 24.

2 Arrange four small flying-geese units, four tan-and-red print 1½" squares, and a red print 2½" square into three horizontal rows. Sew the pieces in each row together and press the seam allowances toward the flying-geese units. Join the rows and press the seam allowances toward the middle row. Repeat to make a total of six star units.

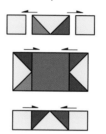

Make 6.

3 Repeat step 1 with the assorted dark 2½" squares and assorted light-tan 2½" x 4½" rectangles to make 24 large flying-geese units.

4 Arrange four large flying-geese units, four assorted light-tan 2½" squares, and one star unit into three horizontal rows. Sew the pieces in each row together and press the seam allowances toward the flying-geese units. Join the rows and press the seam allowances toward the middle row. Repeat to make a total of six blocks.

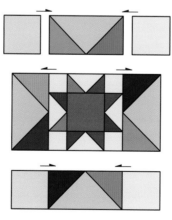

Make 6.

Assemble the Row

Lay out the blocks side by side into one horizontal row. Sew the blocks together. Press the seam allowances open.

A Tisket, a Tasket

Designed by Alma Allen of Blackbird Designs

Finished row: 10" x 48"

Materials

Yardage is based on 42"-wide fabric. Fat quarters are 18" x 21".

1 fat quarter *each* of red floral, red paisley, and red dot for blocks and appliqués

1 fat quarter *each* of cream print and cream check for blocks

Cutting

All measurements include ¼"-wide seam allowances.

From the red floral, cut:

1 square, 6½" x 6½"

4 squares, 6¼" x 6¼"; cut into quarters diagonally to yield 16 triangles

1 square, 4⅜" x 4⅜"; cut in half diagonally to yield 2 triangles (you'll use 1 and have 1 left over)

3 squares, 2⅝" x 2⅝"

From the cream check, cut:

1 rectangle, 9½" x 11½"

1 square, 4⅜" x 4⅜"; cut in half diagonally to yield 2 triangles

6 squares, 2⅝" x 2⅝"

4 rectangles, 2¼" x 4"

4 squares, 2¼" x 2¼"

From the red paisley, cut:

4 squares, 6¼" x 6¼"; cut into quarters diagonally to yield 16 triangles

1 square, 4⅜" x 4⅜"; cut in half diagonally to yield 2 triangles (you'll use 1 and have 1 left over)

4 squares, 2⅝" x 2⅝"

From the red dot, cut:

1 square, 4⅜" x 4⅜"; cut in half diagonally to yield 2 triangles

7 squares, 2⅝" x 2⅝"

(Continued on page 94)

Pieced basket blocks have a long history in quiltmaking. Here, three variations (Flower Basket, Cake Stand, and one simply named Basket) are charmingly interrupted by a single appliquéd blossom.

(Continued from page 93)

From the cream print, cut:

1 square, 4⅜" x 4⅜"; cut in half diagonally to yield 2 triangles
(you'll use 1 and have 1 left over)
9 squares, 2⅝" x 2⅝"; cut *1* square in half diagonally to yield 2 triangles
4 rectangles, 2¼" x 4"
2 squares, 2¼" x 2¼"

Make the Basket Blocks

1 Draw a diagonal line from corner to corner on the wrong side of each cream check and cream print 2⅝" square. Layer a marked cream check square on top of each red floral 2⅝" square and three red dot 2⅝" squares. Layer a marked cream print square on top of the remaining red dot and red paisley 2⅝" squares. Stitch ¼" from each side of the marked lines. Cut the squares apart on the marked lines to make two small half-square-triangle units from each pair (28 total). Press the seam allowances toward the red prints.

| Cream check, red floral. Make 6. | Cream check, red dot. Make 6. | Cream print, red dot. Make 8. | Cream print, red paisley. Make 8. |

2 Using the 4⅜" triangles, sew the cream check triangles to the red floral triangle and one red dot triangle along the long edges to make large half-square-triangle units. Sew one cream print triangle to the paisley triangle in the same manner. Press the seam allowances toward the red prints.

| Cream check, red floral. Make 1. | Cream check, red dot. Make 1. | Cream print, red paisley. Make 1. |

3 Assemble the cream check/red floral small and large units, two cream check 2¼" x 4" rectangles, and two cream check 2¼" squares as shown. Sew the pieces into sections, and then sew the sections together to make an A basket unit. Press the seam allowances in the directions indicated. Repeat with the cream check/red dot units to make a total of two A basket units.

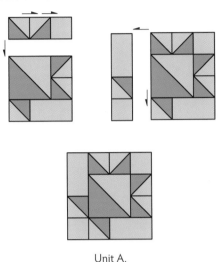

Unit A.
Make 2.

4 Assemble seven cream print/red paisley small units, one matching large unit, two cream print 2¼" x 4" rectangles, and one cream print 2¼" square as shown. Sew the pieces into sections, and then sew the sections together to make one B basket unit. Press the seam allowances in the directions indicated. You'll have one small half-square-triangle unit left over for another project.

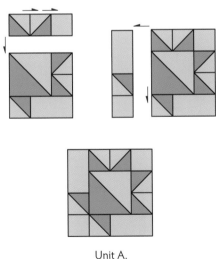

Unit A.
Make 2.

5 Assemble the cream print/red dot small units, the remaining red dot 4⅜" triangle, two cream print 2⅝" triangles, two cream print 2¼" x 4" rectangles, and one cream print 2¼" square as shown on page 96. Sew

the pieces into sections, and then sew the sections together to make one C basket unit. Press the seam allowances in the directions indicated by the arrows.

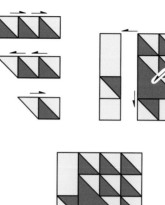

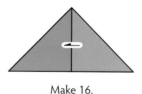

Unit C.
Make 1.

6 Sew each red paisley 6¼" triangle to a red floral 6¼" triangle to make 16 pieced corner triangles.

Make 16.

7 Sew corner triangles to opposite sides of each A, B, and C unit. Press the seam allowances toward the triangles. Repeat on the opposite sides of each unit to complete the basket blocks.

Make the Appliquéd Block

1 Using the patterns on page 97, prepare the shapes for turned-edge appliqué, and make approximately 9" of ½"-wide bias strips from the red floral 6½" square for the stem. (Refer to step 3 of "Make the Appliquéd Strip" for "Garland Knot" on page 70 for instructions on cutting the bias tape from a square.) You can find more information on turned-edge appliqué and making bias stems at ShopMartingale.com/HowtoQuilt.

2 Position the shapes on the cream check 9½" x 11½" rectangle and appliqué in place, referring to the photo on page 93 as needed. When appliqué is complete, press the block and trim to 8½" x 10½".

Assemble the Row

Referring to the photo, lay out the blocks in one horizontal row as shown or as desired. Sew the blocks together. Press the seam allowances open.

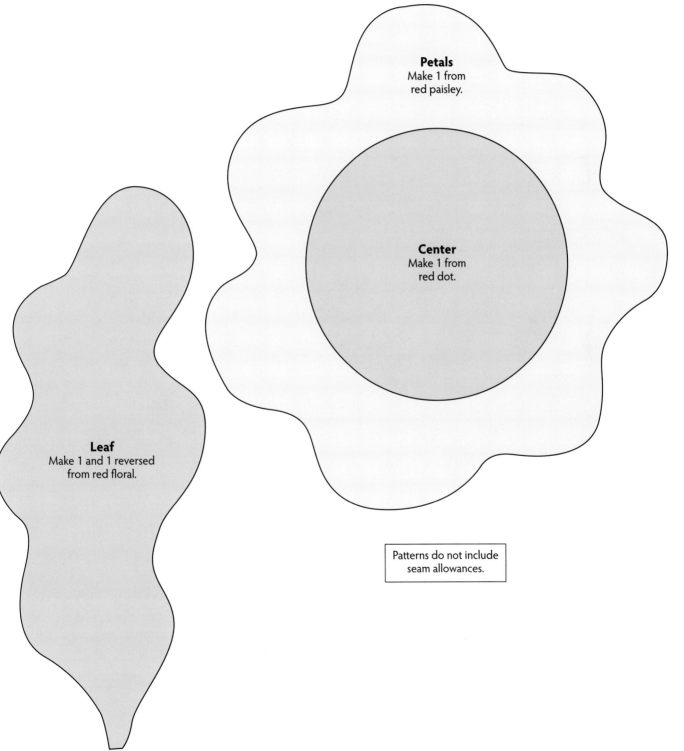

Petals
Make 1 from
red paisley.

Center
Make 1 from
red dot.

Leaf
Make 1 and 1 reversed
from red floral.

Patterns do not include
seam allowances.

Drunkard's Path

Designed by Kaari Meng of French General

A two-color quilt is anything but plain when you keep it scrappy. Practice sewing curves on the gentle waves of Drunkard's Path blocks.

Finished row: 9" x 48"

Materials

Yardage is based on 42"-wide fabric.

⅝ yard *total* of assorted red prints
⅜ yard *total* of assorted cream prints
Template plastic

Cutting

All measurements include ¼"-wide seam allowances. Trace patterns A and B on page 99 onto template plastic and cut them out. Use the templates to cut the block pieces from the fabrics indicated below.

From the assorted red prints, cut a *total* of:
16 squares, 3½" x 3½"
32 A pieces

From the assorted cream prints, cut a *total* of:
32 B pieces

Make the Drunkard's Path Blocks

1 Fold each A and B piece in half and finger-press the fold to mark the centers of the curved edges.

2 With right sides together and centers aligned, pin the pieces together at the centers and ends. Add additional pins between these pins as needed. With the A piece on top, sew the pieces together, easing in the fullness. Press the seam allowances toward the A piece. Repeat to make a total of 32 blocks.

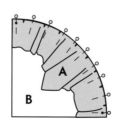

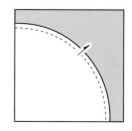

Assemble the Row

Referring to the photo on page 98, arrange the blocks and assorted red 3½" squares into 16 vertical rows of two Drunkard's Path blocks and one 3½" square each. Sew the pieces in each row together. Press the seam allowances in opposite directions from row to row. Join the rows and press the seam allowances in one direction.

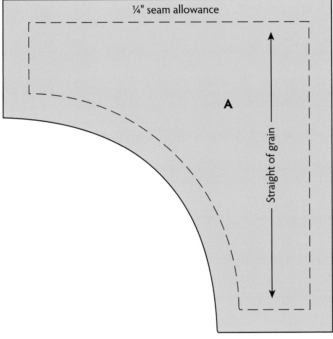

¼" seam allowance

A

Straight of grain

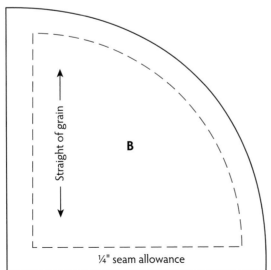

Straight of grain

B

¼" seam allowance

We Are Family

Designed by Joanna Figueroa of Fig Tree and Company

Create a block that stands by itself, but that joins with adjacent blocks when sashed with a chain. The blocks come together as one in a row quilt—like a family!

Finished row: 8" x 48"

Materials

Yardage is based on 42"-wide fabric.

¼ yard _total_ of assorted cream prints for blocks and sashing strips
⅜ yard _total_ of assorted medium and dark prints for blocks
¼ yard of brown print for blocks and sashing strips

Cutting

All measurements include ¼"-wide seam allowances.

From the assorted medium and dark prints, cut a _total_ of:

7 squares, 2½" x 2½" (block centers)
7 sets of 2 matching squares, 2⅞" x 2⅞"; cut in half diagonally to make 4 half-square triangles (28 total) (main star points)
7 squares, 3¼" x 3¼"; cut into quarters diagonally to yield 4 quarter-square triangles (28 total) (secondary star points)

From the assorted cream prints, cut a _total_ of:

6 strips, 1½" x 42"; crosscut into:
    20 rectangles, 1½" x 6½"
    56 squares, 1½" x 1½"
7 squares, 3¼" x 3¼"; cut into quarters diagonally to yield 28 quarter-square triangles

From the brown print, cut:

3 strips, 1½" x 42"; crosscut into 68 squares, 1½" x 1½"

Make the Blocks

1 Lay out two assorted cream 1½" squares and two brown 1½" squares in two horizontal rows of two squares each as shown. Sew the squares in each row together. Press the seam allowances toward the brown. Join the rows to make a four-patch unit. Press the seam allowances in one direction. Repeat to make a total of 28 four-patch units.

Make 28.

2 Select four matching medium or dark half-square triangles for the main star points, four matching medium or dark quarter-square triangles from a different print for the secondary star points, and four assorted cream quarter-square triangles for the star-point backgrounds. Sew each cream quarter-square triangle to a medium or dark quarter-square triangle along the short edges to make a pieced triangle. Press the seam allowances toward the medium or dark. Add a half-square triangle to each pieced triangle to make a star point. Press the seam allowances toward the half-square triangles.

Make 4.

3 Lay out the four star-point units from step 2, four of the four-patch units, and one medium or dark 2½" square in three horizontal rows as shown. Sew the pieces in each row together. Press the seam allowances toward the four-patch units and center square. Join the rows. Press the seam allowances toward the top and bottom rows.

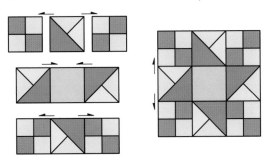

4 Repeat steps 2 and 3 to make a total of seven blocks.

Assemble the Row

1 Alternately lay out the blocks and six cream 1½" x 6½" sashing strips in one horizontal row. Sew the pieces together. Press the seam allowances toward the sashing strips.

2 Alternately join seven cream 1½" x 6½" sashing strips and six brown 1½" squares to make a border strip. Press the seam allowances toward the sashing strips. Repeat to make a total of two border strips. Sew these strips to the top and bottom of the block row. Press the seam allowances toward the border strips.

Blender Rows

Designed by Lissa Alexander of ModaLissa

While all the rows the All-Stars have designed are terrific, if you want to join several of them together in a quilt, you might want to separate some of them with a spacer or blender row. Here you'll find nine options for pieced rows that you can put all together like Lissa did, or use between your favorite rows in the book.

Hourglass Row

Strip Row

Rail Fence Row

Spool Row

Nine Patch Row

X Row

Donut Row

Strip Row

Flying Geese Row

Four Patch Row

HOURGLASS ROW

Finished row: 3" x 48"

Materials

Yardage is based on 42"-wide fabric.

¼ yard of light fabric

¼ yard *total* of assorted medium and dark fabrics

Cutting

All measurements include ¼"-wide seam allowances.

From the light fabric, cut:

1 strip, 4¼" x 42"; crosscut into 8 squares, 4¼" x 4¼". Cut each square
  into quarters diagonally to yield 32 triangles.

From the assorted medium and dark fabrics, cut a *total* of:

8 squares, 4¼" x 4¼"; cut into quarters diagonally to yield 32 triangles

Assemble the Row

1 Sew each light triangle to a medium or dark triangle along the short edges to make a pieced triangle. Press the seam allowances toward the medium and dark triangles. Join two pieced triangles to make a block. Press the seam allowances in either direction. Make 16 blocks.

Make 16.

2 Referring to the photo on page 102, sew the blocks together side by side in one horizontal row, rotating the placement of the background triangles as shown. Press the seam allowances toward the horizontally oriented blocks.

STRIP ROW

Finished row: 2½" x 48"

Materials

Yardage is based on 42"-wide fabric.

1½ yards of light fabric
1½ yards of dark fabric

Cutting

All measurements include ¼"-wide seam allowances.

From the *lengthwise grain* of the light fabric, cut:
1 strip, 1¾" x 48½"
1 strip, 1¼" x 48½"
From the *lengthwise grain* of the dark fabric, cut:
1 strip, 1" x 48½"

Assemble the Row

Sew the light strips to the long edges of the dark strip. Press the seam allowances toward the dark strip.

RAIL FENCE ROW

Finished row: 3" x 48"

Materials

Yardage is based on 42"-wide fabric.

⅛ yard of light fabric
⅛ yard *each* of 2 assorted medium and/or dark fabrics

Cutting

All measurements include ¼"-wide seam allowances.

From the light fabric, cut:
2 strips, 1½" x 42"; crosscut into 16 rectangles, 1½" x 3½"
From *each* of the 2 medium or dark fabrics, cut:
2 strips, 1½" x 42"; crosscut into 16 rectangles, 1½" x 3½" (32 total)

Assemble the Row

1 Sew matching medium or dark rectangles to both long edges of a light rectangle. Press the seam allowances toward the medium or dark rectangles. Repeat to make a total of 16 blocks.

Make 16.

2 Join the blocks side by side in one horizontal row, alternating the colors and the direction of the blocks as shown. Press the seam allowances toward the vertically oriented blocks.

SPOOL ROW

Finished row: 3" x 48"

Materials

Yardage is based on 42"-wide fabric.

⅓ yard of light fabric
16 squares, 4½" x 4½", of assorted medium and dark fabrics

Cutting

All measurements include ¼"-wide seam allowances.

From the light fabric, cut:
1 strip, 2⅜" x 42"; crosscut into 16 squares, 2⅜" x 2⅜"
2 strips, 2" x 42"; crosscut into 32 squares, 2" x 2"
From *each* of the 16 medium and dark squares, cut:
1 square, 2⅜" x 2⅜" (16 total)
2 squares, 1¼" x 1¼" (32 total)

Assemble the Row

1 Draw a diagonal line from corner to corner on the wrong side of each medium or dark 1¼" square. Lay a marked square on one corner of a light 2" square, right sides together. Sew on the marked

line. Trim ¼" from the stitching line. Press the seam allowances toward the corner. Repeat with the remaining marked squares to make a total of 32 folded-corner units.

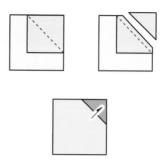

Make 32.

2 Draw a diagonal line from corner to corner on the wrong side of each light 2⅜" square. Layer a marked square on top of a medium or dark 2⅜" square, right sides together. Stitch ¼" from each side of the marked line. Cut the squares apart on the marked lines to make two half-square-triangle units. Repeat with the remaining marked squares to make a total of 32 half-square-triangle units.

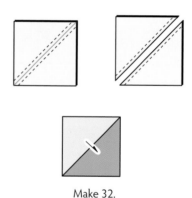

Make 32.

3 Using units made with the same medium or dark fabric, arrange two folded-corner units and two half-square-triangle units into two horizontal rows as shown. Sew the units in each row together. Press the seam allowances toward the spool units. Join the rows. Press the seam allowances in one direction. Repeat to make a total of 16 blocks.

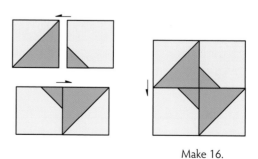

Make 16.

4 Join the blocks side by side in a horizontal row, rotating the blocks so they alternate directions. Press the seam allowances open.

NINE PATCH ROW

Finished row: 3" x 48"

Materials

Yardage is based on 42"-wide fabric.

¼ yard of light fabric
⅛ yard of medium or dark fabric #1
⅛ yard of medium or dark fabric #2

Cutting

All measurements include ¼"-wide seam allowances.

From the light fabric, cut:
3 strips, 1½" x 42"; crosscut into 72 squares, 1½" x 1½"

From medium or dark print #1, cut:
2 strips, 1½" x 42"; crosscut into 40 squares, 1½" x 1½"

From medium or dark print #2, cut:
2 strips, 1½" x 42"; crosscut into 32 squares, 1½" x 1½"

Assemble the Row

1 Lay out five medium or dark #1 squares and four light squares in three horizontal rows as shown. Sew the squares in each row together. Press the seam allowances toward the dark squares. Join the rows to make block A. Press the seam allowances toward the top and bottom rows. Repeat to make a total of eight A blocks.

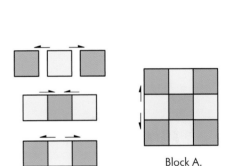

Block A.
Make 8.

2 Lay out five light squares and four medium or dark #2 squares in three horizontal rows as shown. Sew the squares in each row together. Press the seam allowances toward the dark squares. Join the rows to make block B. Press the seam allowances toward the middle row. Repeat to make a total of eight B blocks.

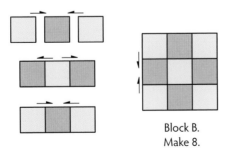

Block B.
Make 8.

3 Alternately join the A and B blocks in one horizontal row. Press the seam allowances toward the A blocks.

X ROW

Finished row: 6" x 48"

Materials

Yardage is based on 42"-wide fabric.

⅜ yard of light fabric
⅜ yard *total* of assorted medium and dark fabrics

Cutting

All measurements include ¼"-wide seam allowances.

From the light fabric, cut:
5 strips, 2" x 42"; crosscut into 96 squares, 2" x 2"

From the medium and dark fabrics, cut a *total* of:
32 squares, 3½" x 3½"

Assemble the Row

1 Draw a diagonal line from corner to corner on the wrong side of each light square. Lay a marked square on opposite corners of a medium or dark 3½" square, right sides together. Sew on the marked lines. Trim ¼" from the stitching lines. Press the seam allowances toward the corners. Repeat on one additional corner. Make a total of 32 units.

Make 32.

2 Lay out four units from step 1 in two horizontal rows of two units each. Sew the units in each row together. Press the seam allowances in opposite directions. Join the rows. Press the seam allowances in one direction. Repeat to make a total of eight blocks.

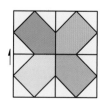

Make 8.

3 Join the blocks side by side in one horizontal row, rotating the blocks so the seam allowances oppose each other. Press the seam allowances open.

DONUT ROW

Finished row: 3" x 48"

Materials

Yardage is based on 42"-wide fabric.

¼ yard of light fabric
⅛ yard of medium or dark fabric #1
4" x 7" rectangle of medium or dark fabric #2

Cutting

All measurements include ¼"-wide seam allowances.

From the light fabric, cut:

3 strips, 1½" x 42"; crosscut into:
    16 rectangles, 1½" x 3½"
    24 squares, 1½" x 1½"

From medium or dark fabric #1, cut:

2 strips, 1½" x 42"; crosscut into:
    16 rectangles, 1½" x 3½"
    16 squares, 1½" x 1½"

From medium or dark fabric #2, cut:

8 squares, 1½" x 1½"

Assemble the Row

1 Sew medium or dark #1 squares to the top and bottom of a light square. Press the seam allowances toward the medium or dark. Add medium or dark #1 rectangles to the sides of this unit to make block A. Press the seam allowances toward the rectangles. Repeat to make a total of eight A blocks.

Block A.
Make 8.

2 Sew white squares to the top and bottom of a medium or dark #2 square. Press the seam allowances toward the medium or dark. Add white rectangles to the sides of this unit to make block B. Press the seam allowances toward the rectangles. Repeat to make a total of eight B blocks.

Block B.
Make 8.

3 Alternately join the A and B blocks, rotating the A blocks so the side seams are vertical and the B blocks so the side seams are horizontal.

FLYING GEESE ROW

Finished row: 3" x 48"

Materials

Yardage is based on 42"-wide fabric.

⅓ yard of light fabric

32 rectangles, 2" x 3½", of assorted medium and dark scraps

Cutting

All measurements include ¼"-wide seam allowances.

From the light fabric, cut:

4 strips, 2" x 42"; crosscut into 64 squares, 2" x 2"

Assemble the Row

1 Draw a diagonal line from corner to corner on the wrong side of each white 2" square. Lay a marked square on one end of a scrap 2" x 3½" rectangle as shown, right sides together. Sew on the marked line. Trim ¼" from the stitching line. Press the seam allowances toward the corner. Lay another marked square on the opposite end of the rectangle as shown; stitch, trim, and press as before to make a flying-geese unit. Repeat to make a total of 32 units.

Make 32.

2 Sew two flying-geese units together along the long edges to make a block. Repeat to make a total of 16 blocks.

Make 16.

3 Join the blocks side by side in one horizontal row with the geese all pointing the same direction. Press the seam allowances toward the points.

FOUR PATCH ROW

Finished row: 3" x 48"

Materials

Yardage is based on 42"-wide fabric.

¼ yard of light fabric
⅛ yard of medium or dark fabric #1
⅛ yard of medium or dark fabric #2

Cutting

All measurements include ¼"-wide seam allowances.

From the light fabric, cut:
2 strips, 2" x 42"; crosscut into 32 squares, 2" x 2"
From medium or dark fabric #1, cut:
1 strip, 2" x 42"; crosscut into 16 squares, 2" x 2"
From medium or dark fabric #2, cut:
1 strip, 2" x 42"; crosscut into 16 squares, 2" x 2"

Assemble the Row

1 Lay out two light squares and two medium or dark #1 squares in two horizontal rows of two squares each. Sew the squares in each row together. Press the seam allowances toward the medium or dark. Join the rows. Press the seam allowances toward the bottom row. Repeat to make a total of eight A blocks.

Block A.
Make 8.

2 Repeat step 1 with the remaining light squares and medium or dark #2 squares to make eight B blocks, pressing the seam allowances toward the top row.

Block B.
Make 8.

3 Alternately sew the blocks together side by side in one horizontal row. Press the seam allowances in one direction.

Here are as many of the All-Stars as we could wrangle in one place.

If my quilting buddies and I were all in a row, we'd be . . .

- laughing, giggling, and looking to see if everyone was standing straight in the row and keeping in their place
- the three wise monkeys
- laughing
- scrappy
- a motley crew
- giggling and encouraging each other (I love them for that!)
- a rather haphazard bunch!
- a formidable group!
- laughing
- happiest lying on a beach!
- passing the bottle of wine
- at a quilt show shopping!
- laughing like crazy!
- wearing stretchy pants
- not sure, but most likely laughing
- encircling the world!
- taking a group photo and some selfies
- small, medium, and large
- giggling
- wearing a lot of patterns
- laughing and joking

Meet the Contributors

Lissa Alexander
ModaLissa.blogspot.com

Alma Allen
Blackbird-Designs.blogspot.com

Lisa Bongean
LisaBongean.com

Barbara Brackman
CivilWarQuilts.blogspot.com

Betsy Chutchian
BetsysBestQuiltsandMore
.blogspot.com

Janet Clare
JanetClare.co.uk

Karla Eisenach
TheSweetwaterCo.com

Joanna Figueroa
FigTreeQuilts.com
FigTreeQuilts.typepad.com

Sandy Gervais
PiecesfromMyHeart.net

Barbara Groves and Mary Jacobson
MeandMySisterDesigns.com

Lynne Hagmeier
KTQuilts.com

Jen Kingwell
JenKingwellDesigns.blogspot.com

Sandy Klop
AmericanJane.com

Kaari Meng
FrenchGeneral.blogspot.com

Carrie Nelson
Blog.ModaFabrics.com

Brenda Riddle
BrendaRiddle.blogspot.com

Camille Roskelley
ThimbleBlossoms.com
CamilleRoskelley.typepad.com

Kathy Schmitz
KathySchmitz.com

Laurie Simpson
MinickandSimpson.blogspot.com

Edyta Sitar
LaundryBasketQuilts.com

Pat Sloan
PatSloan.com

Kate Spain
KateSpain.com
KateSpainDesigns.blogspot.com

Anne Sutton
BunnyHillDesigns.com

Corey Yoder
LittleMissShabby.com